P9-DMC-786

THE
AMNESTY
OF
JOHN DAVID HERNDON

★ ALSO BY JAMES RESTON, JR. ★

TO DEFEND, TO DESTROY

THE
AMNESTY
OF
JOHN DAVID HERNDON

by James Reston, Jr.

McGraw-Hill Book Company

New York   St. Louis   San Francisco   Toronto

959.704
R436

99807

★ FOR DENISE ★

Copyright © 1973 by James Reston, Jr.
All rights reserved.
Printed in the United States of America.
No part of this publication may be reproduced,
stored in a retrieval system, or transmitted, in
any form or by any means, electronic, mechanical,
photocopying, recording, or otherwise, without
the prior written permission of the publisher.

First Edition

123456789BPBP79876543

Library of Congress Cataloging in Publication Data

Reston, James, 1941–
    The amnesty of John David Herndon.

    1. Vietnamese Conflict, 1961–   —Desertions—
United States. 2. Amnesty—United States.
3. Herndon, John David. I. Title.
DS557.A68R48   959.704′31   72–8054
ISBN 0–07–051920–X

Alverno College Library
Milwaukee, Wisconsin

★PRELUDE★

I no longer give the answer with which I tried for so long to soothe the questioners, but chiefly myself: that in Hitler's system, as in every totalitarian regime, when a man's position rises, his isolation increases and he is therefore more sheltered from harsh reality; that with the application of technology to the process of murder the number of murderers is reduced and therefore the possibility of ignorance grows; that the craze for secrecy built into the system creates degrees of awareness, so it is easy to escape observing inhuman cruelties. . . .

I no longer give any of these answers. For they are efforts at legalistic exculpation. . . . In the final analysis, I myself determined the degree of my isolation, the extremity of my evasions, and the extent of my ignorance. . . .

Whether I knew or did not know, or how much or how little I knew is totally unimportant when I consider what horrors I ought to have known about and what conclusions would have been the natural ones to draw from the little I did know. Those who ask me are fundamentally expecting me to offer justifications. But I have none. No apologies are possible.

ALBERT SPEER,
Memoirs of the Third Reich

★INTRODUCTION★

In the fall of 1971 the amnesty issue burst upon the American political scene with a bewildering suddenness. That the tens of thousands of American young men in exile abroad should be pardoned of the "offense" of war resistance and allowed to return to their country was not a new argument. In fact, as early as the Democratic National Convention of 1968, church groups had argued that very point before the Democratic Platform Committee. What was new was the seriousness with which the issue was debated, and the apparent feeling of the many Presidential aspirants at the time that they must have a position on the question.

The mood of the country was, of course, the reason for the issue's emergence, for the American people were led to believe that the war was drawing to a close. President Nixon declared in October 1971 that U.S. Forces were in a "defensive position" in Vietnam. By the winter of 1971–72 the American military force could have been supported wholly by volunteers. Over 60 percent of the American people felt by this time that the war had been a mistake. So how could the government—which was withdrawing from Vietnam because the effort had been a mistake—continue to consider as criminals those who had been saying the war was a mistake all along? How could the American people agree with the conclusions of the young men in exile—that the war was wrong and immoral and that they could not participate in it —and, at the same time, cast these young men off as traitors unwilling to serve their country?

Amnesty has historically been an aspect of the reconciliation of a divided nation. In the Civil War period, the most relevant precedent to our present predicament, Presidents Lincoln and Johnson each twice declared conditional amnesty for the rebels to bring the South and the North back together. But underlying these amnesties from the beginning was the premise that the common Southerner was not to blame for joining the rebel armies. Instead, the presidents felt the commoner had been hoodwinked into rebellion, by the rich, the aristocratic, and the powerful, the Southern leaders. They therefore extended amnesty immediately to the common man, excepting only the leaders from pardon. But on December 24, 1868, in his universal amnesty proclamation, Andrew Johnson recognized that the reconciliation of a nation demanded that even these leaders be pardoned of rebellion.

In the Vietnam era the division is generational rather than geographical. The young have fought and died in the war; only the young have been subject to the draft; only the young have been faced with the agonizing decision of whether they could participate in such an imperial effort. For the rest of the American populace the Vietnam era has brought no particular dislocation. Indeed, it has brought a good measure of prosperity. And so a reconciliation between the generations would be one reason for declaring amnesty, for clearly the young have taken up the exiles' cause. But it would not meet the true thrust of the issue.

Because the chief victims of the war have been young, so the chief resisters to the war have been young. We have had years of turbulence in the streets over the war and the draft. The government has found ways to alleviate that pressure without changing the essential character of the war: it made the draft more equitable with the draft lottery, and now the reduced draft calls have all but defused college anti-war protest. But while campus protest has diminished, resistance within the defense establishment has reached a point where it threatens the viability of a military force: the refusal of entire companies to go out on missions, the drug addiction of thousands of soldiers, the refusal of Captain Howard Levy to demean medicine as a weapon of war, and desertion at the highest rate in American history. There have also been the contributions of low-ranking enlisted men and functionaries to the exposure of American atrocities: a sergeant revealed to the American public the story of My Lai, enlisted men and young officers showed that My Lai was larger but not inconsistent with the pattern of U.S. war crime, a sergeant exposed General John Lavelle's ordering of unauthorized air strikes over North Vietnam; and there were young men who talked about the meteorological warfare of rainstorms over North Vietnam rice fields and the ecological warfare of firestorms in South Vietnam forests, and Daniel Ellsberg, who exposed a decision-making process devoid of human considerations.

Were it not for the existence of the exiles, the Vietnam era might end abruptly with the withdrawal of the last American soldier and the return of the American prisoners, and the American people might hastily go about expunging the memory of this ghastly period from their minds. But the exiles cannot be ignored. They symbolize a nation's wrong turning. They are demanding repatriation without any assumption of wrongdoing on their part. Thus, the Vietnam era will drag on so long as the nation does not take action on their plight that is appropriate to the acknowledgment of the mistaken and even criminal waging of war. So ending that era finally and appropriately, lowering the voices in the argument between the generations, restoring some legitimacy to our institutions, even our military institution, are all reasons for declaring amnesty; but still we have not gone to the true issue.

Will the country be magnanimous in its disappointment? For we are all disappointed by the Vietnam War in one way or another. Some Americans are disappointed that victory was not ours, swiftly and gloriously. Others despair at the moral defeat of the war—the spectacle of the violent, technological bully, vengefully devastating a people and a land abroad and undermining faith in a civilized state at home.

The test of magnanimity will be in the reconstruction of Indochina and the reconstruction of America. The American government's actions toward its dissenters on amnesty will be the clearest and earliest test. So the display of a largeness of spirit in a disappointed nation is also a reason for declaring amnesty; but neither is this the true issue.

The real amnesty issue is the matter of responsibility for what American involvement has brought to the people of Indochina, and what it has done to America as a nation. If this country can face the evidence of the past seven years without avoidance or excuse, if it can recognize what we have become as a result and set about to reclaim our heritage, if it can see the necessity to attend to all the victims of this war in a spirit of obligation, then a universal amnesty for war resistance can come easily, and an end to a long era of recrimination can come early. Thus, true amnesty means the acceptance of the wrong turning, and the dedication to reconstruction and renewal.

Yet at the present time the issue is turned on its head. Those who planned our involvement in Vietnam, who devised our inhuman concepts of devastation, and who executed the technological holocaust are walking free among us and many still hold positions of power. Few are asking if they deserve an amnesty. Only for them would I advocate a conditional amnesty, the condition being that they admit their mistakes. Meanwhile, the young victims in exile who refused to play their game are left to bear the sole legal burden of the war.

This book is about the human dimension of the amnesty problem. It is the story of four men and a woman who came together in a frantic, frightening week in Paris in the early spring of 1972 to dramatize that issue, and of how the American authorities and normal Americans reacted when they returned home. The central figure is a deserter from the American Army, a twenty-four-year-old high-school dropout, an ex-paratrooper and Vietnam veteran, who had been living an uncertain exile in France for two-and-a-half years. Though he was wounded in Vietnam, his mother was to say later, "Most of his battle scars came from his exile after the war." This man made himself available as a test case to face unabashedly the charge of desertion in military court, raising a defense that to desert an army engaged in war crimes is itself no crime. If he succeeded in his challenge, the success would be shared by thousands of other American refugees whom he had left behind in exile. If he failed, he risked five years in jail at hard labor.

The roots of the story extend back to the dialogue on amnesty in the fall and winter of 1971–72. That debate, at least on the political level, avoided the deeper implications of the amnesty question. The politicians were attempting a false balance between the impact of the war on the younger generation and the technical violation by the exiles of either the Selective Service Law by evading the draft, or Article 82 of the Uniform Code of Military Justice by deserting.

Senator George McGovern was the only Presidential candidate in 1971 to take a positive position on amnesty. He perceived, as no other Presidential candidate appeared to, that the American people would elect a postwar president in the fall of 1972, and that his chief task would be to reconcile the nation. Nonetheless, McGovern's proposal for amnesty remained vague as the issue developed. He proposed a general amnesty, meaning a conditional amnesty, in which deserters would be considered for repatriation on a case by case basis.

In contrast, when President Nixon was asked in an October 1971 press conference whether with the withdrawal of American forces from Vietnam he would entertain the notion of amnesty, he clipped a flat, angry "No." It was a blunt and insensitive response, and did much to vitalize an amnesty movement. Articles, including my own, advocating universal, unconditional amnesty appeared; *Newsweek* did a cover story on the question which contained a poll stating that 63 percent of the American people favored a conditional amnesty while only 7 percent favored a universal amnesty; a *Time* essay advocated conditional solution; and Senator Robert Taft of Ohio proposed three years' alternative service for draft evaders with deserters being left to the normal processes of military justice. President Nixon was again asked about the subject on January 17, 1972. This time he hedged a bit more, and his statement became the official government policy:

> The answer is at this time "No." As long as there are Americans who chose to serve their country rather than desert their country, and they are there in Vietnam, there will be no amnesty for those who deserted their country. As long as there are any POWs held by the North Vietnamese there will be no amnesty for those who deserted their country.... I don't say this because I am hardhearted. I say it because it is the only right thing to do. Two-and-a-half million young Americans had to make the choice when they went to serve in Vietnam. Most of them did not want to go.
>
> I imagine most of those young Americans when they went out there did so with some reluctance, but they chose to serve. Of those that chose to serve, thousands of them died for their choice, and until this war is over, and until we get the POWs back, those who chose to desert their country, a few hundred, they can live with their choice. That is my attitude.

The President should have checked with the Pentagon on his figures, for desertion in 1971 had become nearly as American as enlistment in the armed forces. Rather than the few hundred that the President spoke of, in 1971 alone, 98,324 military men had "deserted their country," and tens of thousand of others had either gone underground or into exile to avoid the draft. And yet the President continued to deny the magnitude of his exile problem through the 1972 campaign, insisting that there were only "a few hundred" in exile, and heightening his vindictive tone, saying that granting an amnesty would "make a mockery" of the sacrifices of those who had served in Vietnam.

In a large, vintage office building off New York City's Union Square, an area which has traditionally been the headquarters of groups involved in radical causes, there is a Dos Passosan office which is a chaos of newspapers, books, files, and posters. On the door, a letterhead announcing the Citizens Commission of Inquiry into U. S. War Crimes is scotch-taped to the glass.

In the fall of 1971 the Citizens Commission was a group in search of identity. For two years it had dedicated itself to the cause of exposing American war crimes in Vietnam through a series of conclaves around the country. In these affairs Vietnam veterans testified to atrocities they had seen in the war zone. The Commission had been founded in November 1969, shortly after the My Lai story broke, and the purpose of the inquiries was to show that My Lai was not an isolated accident, but part of a pattern of atrocity which flowed logically and naturally from the kind of war that the American policy planners had devised. These inquiries culminated in two events: the National Veterans Inquiry in Washington, D.C., in December 1970; and the Dellums hearing in April 1971, an unofficial investigation of American war atrocities convened by Representative Ronald V. Dellums of California, but largely organized by the Commission. I knew of the work of the Commission, having attended the National Veterans Inquiry, and I admired it, for I felt deeply that the political and command responsibilities for the personal and technological assault of the American military on the Vietnamese people lay squarely with the highest level of decision-making. The theory behind this activity was that when the American people were informed about the daily atrocities that resulted from American policies they would be shocked and put an end to these policies.

But the war crimes issue spent itself in 1970 and 1971. Six soldiers who were at My Lai were tried. Only Lieutenant William Calley was convicted. Charges against thirteen of fourteen officers for covering up the massacre were dropped. The fourteenth officer, Colonel Oran K. Henderson, was tried and found innocent on the strength of Captain Medina's testimony that he had lied to Colonel Henderson. Medina had told Henderson that "only" twenty-two innocent civilians had been killed at My Lai, when he knew that the figure was at least 130. Twenty-two civilian dead would not have constituted a massacre in American parlance, whereas 130 would have.

There had been efforts in 1970 and 1971 to force the issue

of command responsibility for war crimes. In the case of Sergeant Torres, who was one of the GIs charged at My Lai, his defense counsel, Charles Weltner, raised the question of General William Westmoreland's responsibility for My Lai, claiming that it was the policy of free-fire zones and body counts that had led to the tragedy. Weltner based his charge on the precedent of General Tomoyuki Yamashita, the Japanese military commander in the Philippines whose troops had also run amuck and massacred civilians. Yamashita, even though he had no knowledge of the massacre, since his communications with the berserk unit had been cut, paid for the massacre with his life. He was hanged by the American military in 1945. General Douglas MacArthur said of the case:

> General Yamashita's record was a blot on the military profession. Revolting as this may be in itself, it pales before the sinister and far-reaching implication thereby attached to the profession of arms. *The soldier, be he friend or foe, is charged with the protection of the weak and unarmed . . . . When he violates this sacred trust, he not only profanes his entire cult, but threatens the very fabric of international society.*

But the charges against Torres were dropped and the Pentagon dismissed the countercharge against Westmoreland in an off-hand, one-paragraph statement, saying that Westmoreland did not know about the My Lai massacre until many months after it had occurred—even though he had communicated his congratulations to Company C for the reported body count of 129 the day after.

The year of 1971 ended with a poll by two Harvard professors which indicated that two-thirds of the one thousand Americans interviewed thought that most of their fellow citizens, if ordered, would "shoot all inhabitants of a Vietnamese village suspected of aiding the enemy including old men, women, and children." The study also determined that five out of eight of those interviewed thought Calley should never have been brought to trial for his part in My Lai.

Thus, the government has never admitted responsibility for human devastation in Vietnam, and the American public has never objected. Official Washington had sidetracked the war crimes issue, and even when the Pentagon Papers were released, the embarrassment was never translated into an inquiry into how decisions were made and how that process should be changed.

But the question of amnesty had potential for the revitalization of the debate on war crimes, and the peace issue in general. For universal amnesty—the blanket, unconditional repatriation of all who have gone into exile for war resistance—is founded on the belief that American guilt over Vietnam rests with those who planned the war policies, and no official body can be morally qualified to make conditions or reservations on repatriation for those who refused to participate. Conditional amnesty offers repatriation without the national acceptance of responsibility for war policies. It implies crime, and places the burden of guilt or innocence on the resister rather than on the government. Universal amnesty, on the other hand, states that the Vietnam War has been so destructive not only to that small nation, but to the big one, the United States; and that true reconciliation can only take place if the slate is wiped clean, and we begin anew.

The emotional dynamic of this argument was epitomized by an exchange between Dean Rusk and my wife in a conclave in the spring of 1972 at the Duke University Law School. When she pressed him on amnesty, he said, "What do you want me to do? Say 'I'm sorry. They were right and I was wrong'?"

"That's what universal amnesty is all about," Denise had replied.

"Well you're *never* going to hear that from me!" Rusk said furiously. It was a reply worthy of Bull Connor.

As the amnesty debate took shape, in the winter months of 1971–72, it became clear that the deserter side of the problem (as opposed to the draft-evader side) was going to be the harder to sell to the American people. There were four reasons. First, desertion is more closely connected with treason than is draft evasion. Second, the discipline of the military forces, upon which their viability depends, is thought to be at stake. Third, the American public is not apt to be sympathetic with a soldier who volunteered and later deserted. And finally, and perhaps the most important, deserters tend to be working class, often undereducated and unskilled, and frequently inarticulate about the moral or political nature of their actions, whereas the draft evader is more commonly middle class and college educated, the beneficiary of draft counseling, and articulate about his actions and their motives.

On November 15, 1971, Tod Ensign, the general counsel of the Citizens Commission of Inquiry, received a despairing letter from a draft resister in Paris, stating that the exile community was dwindling and the political movement around the war issue was drying up there. As evidence of this, the letter stated one of the last "old timers" was about to pack his bags and return home. Was there any chance, the letter continued dismally, that CCI might help in contacting a lawyer for his reentry?

Tod Ensign, and his co-worker, Mike Uhl, by this time the last remaining staff of CCI, saw the political possibilities of this request immediately. Here was a chance to combine the amnesty and the war-crimes issues with a test case on desertion and exile. They went into long discussions and in December 1971 changed their organizational name to "Safe Return," a "committee in support of self-retired veterans [deserters]."

Safe Return's contacts in the exile community were superb, since Mike and Tod had taken many depositions from deserters abroad on the war-crimes issue. But casting for the role of a test case is serious business both for the director and the actor. If the director is poor, the actor in this case could get five years at hard labor. If the actor is poor, the production would fall flat politically. Thus, the success of a test case would have to be a delicate balance of the human and the political, and Safe Return was not going to jump into anything too quickly.

In December 1971 I received a telephone call from Mike Uhl asking if I was interested in doing a book on the return of a deserter. I had first met Mike in Washington two years before at the National Veterans Inquiry, where he was the calm, professional contact for the Inquiry. He is of a new breed of anti-war organizer: replete with the radical analysis of the ills of American society, convinced that the Vietnam War is the epitome of those ills, and adept at stage-managing events that capture wide press coverage.

At twenty-eight, Mike's commitment to the movement was based on personal experience. He had been an intelligence officer in Quang Ngai Province, the free-fire zone where My Lai is situated. His unit was the 11th Brigade of the American Division, commanded at that time by Colonel John W. Donaldson, who later was charged with "gook-hunting" from his helicopter. Before his war experience, Mike had ambitions of becoming a diplomat, having graduated from Georgetown University, a spawning-ground for diplomats, in 1967. His instinct thus was to keep his record clean. But in Vietnam, he realized after two weeks of his tour the impossibility of the task to which he was assigned: to collect intelligence on enemy troop movements. The sources that his unit was paying for information were completely untrustworthy, tided over simply by the piasters that the Americans gave them for information that was impossible to verify. Nonetheless, the Air Force and artillery liaisons to the Brigade came to Mike daily for information upon which they could initiate strikes, for they had a daily requirement of a set number of strikes. Mike passed on the information from the sources, openly marking it "unreliable," and the strikes went forward. Furthermore, Mike had often witnessed the use of torture in interrogations, both by the Vietnamese and the Americans, and had testified about them in the National Veterans Inquiry. Thus, he had experienced in his flesh the impossible moral position into which so many young Americans have been forced in this war.

Three months into his Vietnam tour, Mike contracted tuberculosis. He has often wondered whether the disease was somehow self-induced. For two months more, plagued by a worsening cough, his senses dulled and emotions drained by his horror at the war, his mind leading him to identify with Michele in Gide's *Immoralist*, he lay around in his hootch and made no pretense of performing intelligence duties. In the end he was flown out of Vietnam after five months there and released from the Army with a 100-percent disability. Now, while his speech is laced with the terms of political radicalism, his staying power stems from a Vietnam hootch, and the political techniques he uses against the military are often the techniques that the military taught him. Vietnam remains the point of focus in his political outlook which "brings everything together."

In the telephone call, Mike explained to me that they had not decided on the method of reentry for the deserter, but they were considering two options: (1) a covert reentry, with the deserter popping up around the country at antiwar rallies *à la* Daniel Berrigan; or (2) an open reentry, returning the deserter to military custody, and a visible struggle against the charge of desertion in military court, raising a defense, based on U.S. war crimes in Vietnam.

Mike's proposal intrigued me greatly, not only because this appeared to be a dramatic way to force the amnesty issue on the military and the country at large, but also because it would be an opportunity for me to acquaint myself with the exile community whose cause I had taken up. I had been writing about amnesty at that point for nearly a year, and in the fall of 1971 was one of a number trying to get off the ground a national amnesty organization that would be politically charged, whose task it would be to force amnesty as a major issue in the 1972 Presidential campaign. I felt that amnesty was, first and foremost, important to the dignity and self-respect of a postwar America and, secondarily, a humanitarian effort to help the victims in exile. The Safe Return suggestion was an opportunity for me to personalize the issue.

In a somewhat cloak-and-dagger correspondence that followed, Safe Return indicated that they were considering three men for their first case, all in exile in a "European capital" that I first assumed was Stockholm. First was X, later called Bill, a Vietnam vet of Appalachian background from a city "below the Mason-Dixon line," an airborne sergeant who had deserted in Germany when the Army tried to send him back to Vietnam for a second tour. The problem with Bill was that he was unstable. The second was called "Paco," a twenty-three-year-old Puerto Rican, sensitive and intelligent, an ex-Marine who had deserted in Okinawa on the way to Vietnam and had lived underground in Japan for two years before he relocated to Europe. The third was called "Barry," an ex–Green Beret and dropout from a Catholic college, who refused orders to Vietnam and gave interviews to California media on his anti-war views when he was on leave. At Fort Bragg a court-martial was convened, but before it could try Barry, he fled to Canada and then to Europe. The problem with Barry was that he was on drugs. Of the three, X's (or Bill's) adjustment to foreign exile had been the toughest.

I replied to this correspondence saying I thought the covert reentry and Daniel Berrigan strategy were unrealistic, since the deserter would not have resources comparable to Berrigan's, and that I favored the open challenge. Furthermore, I told Safe Return that of the three men mentioned, X or Bill, seemed the best man for the first case. His Vietnam tour would undermine the argument—always made but never supported—that deserters were cowards or traitors who simply could not face combat. A deserter with combat experience could most dramatically make the case for amnesty, I felt. That X might be unstable did not bother me. What could you expect after all he's been through? I wrote Mike and Tod.

The problem with the open challenge was, I said, that "X is likely to get it in the end." I could not conceive of a situation where a deserter, admitting desertion openly in military court, could overcome the charges against him by arguing that the whole Vietnam enterprise was criminal. Both military and civilian courts had never taken this argument seriously throughout the Vietnam era, not in the Levy case or the Spock case or the hundreds of draft resistance cases. Were we thus toying with a human life, already tragically dislocated enough by exile, for a selfish, political goal? Mike and Tod accepted the possibility of an eventual conviction, but were confident in their ability to embarrass the military sufficiently that their defense would redound to their client's interest. "We burned them on war crimes, and we can burn them on this too," Mike said and pointed out that X's intention was to give himself up to military authorities anyway. And yet the military's choice when confronted with a test case was clear: they could either treat a politically charged case gingerly, avoiding a public outcry, or they could accept the challenge, and make an example of the deserter that would horrify other deserters.

In late December 1971 I went to Safe Return's office in New York to talk over the possibilities. Mike had added a Leninesque goatee since I had seen him last and wore denim pants and jacket, with a Greek corduroy sailor cap on his head. It was a uniform that was to be his standard in the week we were to spend in Paris that spring, and once during the week, when he made contact with a newspaperman, he was to describe himself over the phone as "tall and thin and dressed like a cowboy"—but whoever heard of a cowboy with a Greek cap and a frizzy haircut and well-kept goatee, unless it was in the East Village, where Mike, in fact, lives?

Mike introduced me to Tod Ensign. Tod had come to the Veterans movement in a more roundabout way. He had not become politically active until he was a law student in Wayne University in Detroit, after graduating from Michigan State. Detroit in the years 1963–66 was "pre-riot" and a lively city of varying political and cultural currents. Tod looks upon these years as a "growing time." He became involved with SNCC and went to the Selma March; he attended a Saul Alinsky training program and got into tenant organizing; as a law student, he defended indigent clients in misdemeanor cases. In 1966 upon his graduation from Wayne, with the war escalating at a leapfrog rate, Tod was determined not to serve. Then twenty-five years old, he had one more year of draft vulnerability. Thus, taking the legal option that so many of his generation had taken, he entered a one-year L.L.M. program at New York University to get him past the twenty-six-year-old cut-off point for the draft.

During that year in New York, he worked part time in legal matters for Mobilization for Youth on the Lower East Side, all the time developing his "political analysis" and becoming alienated from the liberal and radical lawyers who, he said, were not organizing for basic change. Nonetheless, after N.Y.U. he tried poverty law and joined O.E.O. in legal services as their "resident radical," working very hard, making $14,000 a year and squandering it easily, starting to drink too much, feeling tired and drained and frustrated as a government bureaucrat.

After a year and a half of this, Tod decided he had to get out. He was accepted in a Rutgers Ph.D. program, which, he said, offered the prospect of comfort for a lifetime as a lawyer-Ph.D., making fat fees for consulting jobs. And then he went off on a trip to Africa. He attended the Pan African Conference in Algiers and continued on to Mali and Senegal. Off Dakar, Senegal, Tod visited the Isle de Gorée, a slave transshipment point where the slave ships docked right in a fortress, and the slaves were pushed directly through holes in the stone floors into the holds. The experience had an emotional effect on him, and when he went back to New York, he decided not to return to Rutgers. He became involved in various leftist organizations in New York, and ended up as a founder of the Citizens Commission of Inquiry.

Mike occasionally calls their effort together the "Mutt-and-Jeff routine." The phrase comes from military intelligence parlance as well as the comic strips, referring to the nice guy–tough guy technique used in the interrogation of prisoners. But there is a certain physical reality to the phrase also, for Tod at thirty-two has started to contend with a carbohydrate diet. In Paris he was to dress on the chic side, sometimes with pants bloused into riding boots. With his round face, long hair, and olive skin, he looked something like a cossack. With Tod's legal and administrative skills and Mike's direct experience with Vietnam, coupled now with two years of organizing war-crimes inquiries, they are an effective pair.

On February 24, 1972, a time when I was lecturing on amnesty in California, Tod wrote a letter to X, asking him if he was prepared to come home as the first test case on amnesty for deserters, and informing him that I was interested in making him the central figure of a book. This letter was to take on great significance in the week of March 13–20. Plans were made to go to Paris during the spring break at the University of North Carolina but still there was no response from X. Tod and Mike tried to convince me that if X was not prepared to come back, that there were other possibilities for the test case. But I insisted on an escape clause from the agreement. I had to see for myself if X was the right person and further, if X were the man, I needed to be sure that he was going into a relationship with Safe Return with his eyes open.

In retrospect, it seems to me that we embarked upon this adventure with the purpose of a test case grossly undefined. What did we expect to gain: Sympathy for deserters? (Would the American people ever have sympathy for them?) A broader appreciation of the amnesty issue? Embarrassment of the military? What did we hope for in a military trial? These fundamental questions were curiously never discussed. Success itself was never defined. Nor did we consider the price of failure.

On Sunday, March 12, 1972, Mike, Tod, and I flew overnight from New York to London, and on Monday hopped over to Paris. We collapsed at a small hotel in the Rue des Ecoles in the Latin Quarter for four hours. At eight o'clock Monday night we gathered again in a tiny Vietnamese restaurant several blocks from the hotel. Over Fish Laquer with *nuoc mam*, I learned for the first time that X was John David Herndon from Baltimore.

★RETURN★

Somebody tapped you on the shoulder and said come along son we're going to war. So you went. But why? In any other deal even like buying a car or running an errand you had the right to say what's in it for me? Otherwise you'd be buying bad cars for too much money or running errands for fools and starving to death. It was a kind of duty you owed yourself that you should stand up and say look mister why should I do this, for who I am doing it and what am I going to get out of it in the end? You haven't even the right to say yes or no or I'll think it over. There are plenty of laws to protect guys' money even in war time but there's nothing on the books says a man's life's his own.

DALTON TRUMBO,
Johnny Got His Gun

★ TUESDAY, MARCH 14, 1972 ★

The *métro* rose from the depths after Jussieu and became elevated as we rumbled toward Nationale. It was not a long ride from our hotel in the Latin Quarter, about fifteen minutes, but we were already a half-hour late. Perhaps we had come all the way across the ocean, starting in the countryside of Piedmont North Carolina, ending up in the slums of South Paris, only to find that he had gone out. The message had said we would be there at 5 P.M. and had been sent to him that morning by *pneumatique*, that marvelous invention which sucked letters around the city by pneumatic tube and delivered them by messenger in a matter of a few hours. The system was completely dependable—which we were not being.

Nationale is a stop in the 13e Arrondissement, a stop known traditionally as one for the poor people of Paris, an arrondissement where the French Government in the twentieth century has attempted its peculiar kind of urban renewal. After the First World War, the authorities made fleeting attempts to build projects for its working people, dim, depressing structures made of yellowish brick turned to gray with age and soot. *"Habitations à bon marché,"* they were called popularly—cheap housing—though the official name is *"Habitation loyers modérées,"* or moderate-rent housing. Their only conveniences are communal toilets in the hallways and a communal garbage disposal. No hot water, no heat. Most of the rooms have no bathing facilities, so that one must either pay for a bath at a community center or bathe in a drainless apartment and swab up the water afterwards. And yet the competition to get into one of these projects is fierce. One has to know someone to accomplish it, for the inducement is the "moderate" rent: for two rooms without bath, toilet, hot running water, or heat, it is less than one hundred francs a month, or $20. We were headed for one of these "apartments."

As we approached Nationale, the newer efforts at rehabilitation were apparent. Amid the cramped, pastel houses, highrise towers called *"tours,"* were popping up all over, some thirty stories high, rising out of vacant lots where once there had been nineteenth-century slums. The old residents of the area had been driven out. They had gone to the suburbs, reversing the American pattern. Rent in the *tours* began at one thousand francs a month. So Nationale is a neighborhood in transition, and it was about to lose another of its poorer residents.

I suggested to Tod that we take a cab, and he agreed. The name of the street was strange. "Strahu" was written in his address book, and I questioned him about it, because it certainly didn't look French to me—more Hungarian or Slavic. We showed it to a cab driver; he shrugged his shoulders. "Connais pas"; to another, the same reaction. But in a bar across from the station someone directed us up several blocks, not far away. We followed his directions and found nothing. In another bar, packed with men in paint-stained work clothes, the bar owner looked in a dog-eared street guide. Sure enough, there was a Rue Sthrau. The bar owner and several customers took great interest in attempting to pronounce the name. We caught another cab. The driver turned to us quizzically, saying, "Petite rue, non?", but finally managed to find it.

The street was narrow and cobblestoned. On one side was a hard dirt park with a swing and a park bench with a few bums draped over it; on the other side, the brick face of the project. Through the iron gate to No. 5, we emerged into a cement courtyard with a single tree in the middle and eight stories of brick rising on three sides and laundry hanging from rope strung between the balconies. Tod looked at his book again for the apartment number—68—and Mike's directions—staircase in the back, left.

As we started off again, a girl came out from a stairwell entrance and walked toward us. She was plainly dressed, a musty tan camel-hair coat held tightly around her, and orange bobby socks above laced saddle shoes. She was homely at first sight—angular features, large bug-eyes, hair pulled straight back and gathered in a long pony tail at the back. She had the disheveled look of the late fifties about her. Her strength and even beauty were to become apparent only later in the week.

"Annette," Tod called out to her. "Hello."

They shook hands. Tod apologized about our lateness and explained our problems in finding the place. He introduced me. "I've forgotten your last name," he said to her. She pronounced it in perfect English; yet it was a French name. Annette, as I will call her, is half French and half American.

"Is John still here?" Tod asked.

"Oh, yeah," she said. "He wanted to stay so he'd be sure not to miss you. I was just going out for some food."

We walked up the six flights in darkness, since pressing the light switch added to the collective electric bill of the stairwell. Annette knocked on the door. "John," she said softly.

The door opened and silhouetted against the glare from the naked light bulb which hung from the kitchen ceiling was John David Herndon. I'm not sure what I expected. I knew he had been born in West Virginia, that his parents had taken him to Baltimore when he was a baby, that his father was a truck driver. I knew that he had volunteered as a paratrooper at the age of eighteen, was in Vietnam for fifteen months, and was wounded during the Tet offensive. And I knew he was a deserter who had been in exile for two-and-a-half years. I was told that he was unstable. But such knowledge does not paint a picture of a human being.

He was thin and gaunt; his hair was combed up in a

pompadour; he was unshaven, though the stubble did not cover a scar that sliced across his cheek from his ear lobe. He talked to Tod in fitful, clipped sentences, almost military sentences, the speech of urgency. And he looked at me suspiciously with quick sidelong glances—glances that I'd come to expect from mountain people after a previous summer in Eastern Kentucky. He wore a blue V-neck sweater, a pair of jeans, and high jackboots with Ben Franklin buckles. It was a uniform that was never to change in that frantic week in Paris.

We sat down at the table. It and three wooden chairs were the only furniture in the barren room. They rested on a cement floor. Along the wall was a coal heater that had not been hooked up with a pipe, and a gas stove with two burners and an oven. On the table was a pot of dried-up noodles and some empty glasses with red rings around the bottoms. The room smelled of stale food and cat litter. John offered us some wine from a plastic bottle and pushed the glasses toward us.

"I hate to tell you this, John," Tod said, "but they've busted you from sergeant to private."

"The bastards," John said, and he looked genuinely hurt by the news.

After a few minutes of conversation about how and what John was doing, he turned to Tod.

"Me and Annette have talked it over," he said, "and I'm ready to go whenever you are." He said it in a rather bland, offhand way, tossing it off as if it were one subject among a thousand. But it was what Tod and I had come 3000 miles to hear.

It was to be the decision that set into motion a vital step in an American odyssey that had begun a quarter of a century before in Monongah, West Virginia—the journey of a man buffeted about in the hold of a society, used by that society, nearly killed by it, discarded and rejected by it, only to begin a new and strange buffeting of exile. But the return was to be a kind of triumphal revenge—perhaps a fleeting moment of victory before doggedly returning to the hold, perhaps a permanent change of style.

Tod left, so I could be alone with John, and we began to talk. "What's it going to be," John asked. "A question-and-answer kind of thing? I've done that before." I said yes, but we had a week, and we'd be talking a lot, so he was to relax.

"I guess you want her here," he said. "We've lived together for over a year, so she might be able to contribute something."

"Fine," I said.

John Herndon's roots go back to the small mining town of Monongah. His father, James Herndon, had been a tank driver in World War II, and after eight months of combat in Europe, had been in one of the first tanks to meet up with the Russians fifty miles from Berlin. When James returned to Monongah, he tried various jobs. His father owned a "one-horse sawmill," and James drove a truck for him hauling mining props; he worked in the mines himself for a short time; and he worked as a mechanic in Monongah. Shortly after his return home, he married Josephine Morris, who had been a waitress in the Palace Restaurant—a "bourgeois restaurant," John called it—in nearby Fairmont.

On April 29, 1947, the local doctor was called to the Herndon house for a "home delivery." It cost the Herndons $35, and John was born. When he was three, in 1950, with the job situation in West Virginia worsening with the automation in the mines, his father was faced with two choices: either to go into the mining prop business full time or migrate to the city. James Herndon felt his wife was too young for a logging camp, and he decided on the latter course. They moved to Baltimore and settled in Victory Villa, a neighborhood of small, boxlike houses thrown up quickly during the war to house the workers for the nearby Martin Marietta plant, which was producing B-26s. A number of other mountain migrants had settled there. James Herndon went to work as a truck driver, and for eight years was "over the road" on long trips.

But when John was eleven, his father went local in Baltimore City, for he felt his son was now at the age where he needed paternal companionship more. The Herndons had always spent time together when James Herndon was home on a seventy-two-hour layover. But now there was more time for the family to go hunting and fishing together.

John was perfect in attendance but "funky" in grades through Victory Villa Elementary School and Middle River Junior High. Into his adolescence he was losing interest, and after one year of Oak Ridge Senior High, he dropped out.

"About 15 percent dropped out of school the year I did," he said. "The majority of the men went into the service. The girls dropped out to get married or because they were pregnant, and a lotta guys dropped out because they had caused it and were trying to get away from it."

The day he dropped out, he went to work at Bata Shoe Company in Belcamp, Md., twenty-two miles away. He worked there nine months on the assembly line, often working sixteen to eighteen hours a day for the overtime. Then he got a better job at Meade Container Company, a corrugated paper factory where he made $1.25 an hour plus commission.

John's leisure time revolved around cars. His father gave him a '51 Ford automatic with a "flat head V-8 engine" when he turned sixteen, and put the registration and insurance in John's name to teach him responsibility. John spent a good deal of time working on the interior in the driveway of the family house. His father bought him a new set of snow tires for the car, and in thirty days they were bald. James Herndon took the tires back to the dealer who simply shook his head. "Give me five bucks and I'll give you a new set of tires," the dealer had said. "They must've been defective, 'cause there's no way those tires could get bald in thirty days."

John's chief memory of the '51 Ford was the time he let a girl drive on a dirt road which was the local lover's lane. She had sunk it into a swamp "right up to the rocker panels." James Herndon had come by in a pickup, and had rousted out about fifteen local boys who were parking that night to help push the car out of the mud. It was not the only time the car had been in the mud, however. On rainy days John had occasionally driven the car up to Delaware back country where he knew about a hard surface road that deadended into an old corn field. John would race the '51 Ford toward the field at 50 m.p.h. and go skidding into the mud. It was, he said, "practice for winter driving."

The '51 gave way to the '56 which John wrecked after hitting an oil slick, which gave way to a '59. John did a good bit of cruising in them all. But he was no "street-corner boy," his parents told me later. His father knew all the hangouts, and if John didn't come home James Herndon would start on the rounds. And the only trouble John had ever been in with the cars was a "speeding ticket": going twenty-five m.p.h in a thirty m.p.h. zone. He managed to get off. Nonetheless, his father used to tell me later, if there was one phrase that sums up John at that age, it was "easily led."

When he was seventeen, John and a friend took off for California in the '59 Ford. Why had he gone?

"It was simple. I was fed up. It was time to go." "Fed up" was an explanation that I was often to get for John's actions.

The teenagers ran out of money in Lake of the Ozarks, Arkansas. John worked as a carpenter there for a few days to earn gas money, and they moved on. In Meade, Kansas, they were picked up for vagrancy, but were released. But in Mineola, Kansas, they ran out of gas. The police picked them up again. This time a call was put in to Baltimore. It turned out that John's companion was underage. James Herndon got in his car and drove eighteen hours straight to Kansas. He sold the '59 Ford to an old lady in Wichita for $150. John remembered his father saying, "O.K., independent, get over here and drive." John had driven most of the way back to Baltimore.

Shortly afterwards, he enlisted in the Army as airborne unassigned.

It has often been said about the anti-war dissidents within the Army (the deserters, or the C.O. applicants, or the letter writers), especially if they were volunteers, that they had no room to gripe, for they had chosen the military of their own free will. The same argument is made by the opponents of amnesty, who reserve their greatest objections for deserters, as opposed to draft evaders. But it is a difficult matter to judge where John Herndon's free will came into his actions.

"I knew I had a six-year obligation anyhow," he said. "I

wanted to travel. I thought I might as well take advantage of it. So I did. I was young. I really didn't know what was going on. I'd read a little about the glamour of the thing, had seen a few paratrooper movies on television. I was what they call gung-ho. Jump school was rough—I'll admit that. It was a real challenge to see what you could take physically. After jump school was over with, I finally ended up in Vietnam, still gung-ho you know, the old paratrooper routine. Found out it wasn't what it was cracked up to be.

"They got their six years. They sure did. Not all of it was active duty, but they got their six years."

Most deserters, informed people say, are likely to be dropouts, who went into the military younger than was necessary, and had a gut reaction either against military life generally, or the war in particular.

John Herndon took his basic training and advanced infantry training at Fort Gordon, Georgia, and went through jump school at Fort Benning, Georgia. His first orders were to the 199th Light Infantry Brigade, a non-airborne unit. In October 1966 he went to Vietnam with the 199th.

"The brigade went over in five C-130s. It's a propeller plane and you can't see out. It took us twenty-eight hours from Lawson Field in Fort Benning to Bien Hoa Air Force Base, with stops in Anchorage, Alaska; Tokyo, Japan; and Okinawa, just looking at the guy across from you. And then they open up the doors at Bien Hoa, and the heat comes rushing in and caresses you. You can't breathe, and you say, 'Jee-zus, I'll never be able to last out here a year, not with this heat! You suffer about two weeks until you get acclimatized. Then it didn't bother me at all.

"We assembled out there on the airfield, a few thousand men, and General Westmoreland gave us a nice big speech that I didn't care too much for. He got us together and said, 'O.K., men, you're all over here to spend one year. Now, some of you are not going home, and a lot of you are going to end up in the hospital, but you're over here to do one thing and that is fight!' And then some colonel got up there and said, 'And we do like big body counts!' That was the end of the ceremony."

John was only supposed to go over to Vietnam with the 199th and then be assigned to an airborne unit, since he was airborne qualified. And, indeed, after the welcoming ceremony, he was sent to the 90th Replacement Station, and on to the 101st Airborne Brigade at Phan Rang. (The 101st was not yet a division then.) But his shipping orders said the 199th on them, and he was summarily shipped back to the 199th. It was the first of many bureaucratic buffetings. Caught up in the "gung-ho" spirit of the airborne soldier, but, more important, wanting the extra $55 jump pay to which he was entitled, John hoped for an airborne assignment, but it would be eight months before he acted on this desire.

In the next eight months he "worked out of the 199th" in the Mekong Delta, first as a team leader, then as a squad leader and as a machine gunner. He rose to buck sergeant. In that period he saw combat eleven times, but it was his first patrol that he remembered best.

"When I first went over, I was stupid. I was a young recruit. As the military teaches you, I was there to stop the flow of Communism in Southeast Asia. So I went with this in mind. I went out on my first patrol. The captain sent five guys about three thousand meters away to check out a tree line. And what they call a VC Killer Squad came out—got 'em all. One guy was crying over the radio, kept hollering out, 'Give us some support. Give us some support!' This captain sat there, he wouldn't let the rest of the company go anywhere. Sat right there on his ass and said there's nothing we can do. That was the first time I went out. I was turned against it at that time. I figured, 'They're going to send people like *him* over here to lead people like us? What kind of an establishment is this? Is this the kind of person I want to work with?' "

While he was with the 199th, he was to see techniques of interrogation by American and Vietnamese that were testified to time and again in the National Veterans Inquiry into U.S. War Crimes.

"At that time they used to use the helicopter quite a bit. They'd take three in a helicopter and interrogate 'em. If they refused to answer, the interrogator would snatch ahold of one of 'em and throw him out and the rest of 'em would chatter away. That was the most effective means of interrogation. I think that kind of thing started in the 5th Special Forces a long time back. When MACV was over there in an advisory capacity in the early sixties. I witnessed that technique in the 199th. I went up as security, because I was a machine gunner. I went up so these people wouldn't get brave and throw the interrogator out of the helicopter—which occasionally happens."

And he'd seen electric torture used in the 199th, just as Mike Uhl had seen it as an intelligence officer.

"They bring a guy in; supposedly he needs medical care. 'Course he's laying there on a stretcher. They have a hand generator-type thing, with two wires comin' out of it . . . and they hook him up . . . . Well, usually down by the balls is how it works. It's pretty efficient there. Anyway, while the medic is patching him up, the interrogator is talking to him, see, and you got some Spec 4 back there crankin' . . . . And that's when the guy's goin' to talk . . . . I was in a tent when I saw it. I don't even think the guys knew I was watchin'. I had a little cold over there, and the medic was my friend. I went into the tent to grab some medicine off of him, and they were twistin' away on this dude, and he was hollerin' and screamin'. So I just kept it to myself 'n' turned around and walked out. I knew what was goin' on. They usually try to make sure that there's not too many people involved when they're doin' something like that. I imagine if it got out, somebody'd really get burned . . . ."

The traditional war went on . . . and the killing.

"Yeah I killed a few people. I won't say I had to do much. The majority of the time you just shot into a certain area, and you didn't know if anybody was there or not. And even if you knew someone was there, you didn't know if you killed 'em. So it's hard to say. But there were three or four instances I know of.

"There are some guys over there who actually enjoy it. You'd think they were insane, collecting ears and eyeballs and things like that. But every time I shoot a person, it just turns my stomach inside out. I'm a complete nervous wreck. You figure he's a human just like you, even though you don't speak the same language. He's doing the same thing you're doing, because somebody told him to do it, and somebody told you to do it. It don't mean you don't like him, and he don't like you."

John told me of the sweeps through villages which have ceased to shock the American public.

"After we went in and checked a village, yes, we'd see a lot of civilian casualties. And then, of course, the American troops, they'd go in and burn down the hooches, destroy the livestock, chickens, and ducks."

"Did you ever do that personally?" I asked.

"Oh, yes."

"How does it happen?"

"Some E-5 says: 'I received orders from up top, and they said, "Level it." ' And sometimes you go into a combat situation, and they'll say, 'Everything's free game. If it walks, if it talks, destroy it.' I've heard that. But it never came from an officer. It always came from an NCO, y' see. Somebody'd told him from above.... And when I was an NCO, I always got the word from an NCO higher than me, never from a company commander."

After eight months of this, John Herndon submitted a 1049 form for a transfer to an airborne unit. He was called in by an NCO and informed that there was an opening in the 5th Special Forces, where he would be able to draw his jump pay. Would he like to go?

"Sounds good," John said.

" 'Well, to go to the 5th Special Forces Group, it's going to require a reenlistment of a year or an extension,' the NCO said. So I got conned into reenlisting for another year."

He was sent to the 5th Special Forces and there served in an advisory capacity with the 33rd Vietnamese Ranger Group in Long Binh and the 44th Vietnamese Ranger Group in Tuy Hoa.

"Actually," he said, "We didn't do anything. We'd go out on patrol with 'em. The area we were working was relatively safe anyway."

With these units he witnessed the Vietnamese interrogation methods.

"The Vietnamese have their own way of interrogating

prisoners. They take one person, and they'll gang him. Beat the shit out of him. Break half his bones in his body, and then when the guy says, 'Yeh, I'm a VC,' they'll take a knife and go swish, swish, VC across his chest, and send him back. That I didn't care so much for, whatsoever. But, I mean, there was nothing I could do about it at that time."

But after only two months with the 5th Special Forces, he was abruptly and without explanation shipped back to the 199th. John's comment on this treatment was, "They say you have a good sex life in the Army. You get it once a day, every day, all day long." But his extra reenlistment time would hold.

Back at the 199th, John went over to see the reenlistment sergeant for an explanation. The sergeant said that he had had nothing to do with John being sent back, and that he had fulfilled his part of the reenlistment contract by sending him up to 5th Special Forces. "They beat around the bush, and finally you say, Hell with it. I got to go anyways."

John submitted another 1049 form shortly after his return and was granted transfer to a security guard unit in Saigon. Through a friend in personnel he managed to get orders there for flight pay, which was the same $55 a month as jump pay.

"A lotta funny things went on over there. If somebody wanted a medal, he'd go to see a buddy in personnel; give him $20 or $10; they'd type him up a set of orders on the medal. Really ridiculous. An infantryman's the only one's supposed to have a combat infantryman's badge. But if somebody wanted one, he'd go out with an infantry unit one time, and they'd type up orders, regardless of whether he'd seen combat or not. I've seen guys go up for a court-martial for black-marketing and some major'd rip up the orders and say 'Don't worry about it, boy,' 'cause he'd be out there making money black-marketing too, see."

John was assigned to guard a POW camp in Bien Hoa, supposedly a model camp that was often visited by dignitaries from the States. Instead of the tiger cages discovered by Don Luce in Con Son, the camp had the "box."

"They were small metal containers which had been used

to ship stuff to Vietnam—metal boxes about six feet tall and four feet wide. The prisoner was kept in them if he was bad or he'd been beaten."

"Were they out in the sun?"

"Yeah, they had to be, to be effective."

John had stood guard at the gate, checking for "unauthorized items," examining the rice ration that was brought in to see that nothing was embedded in it. In some way, he appeared to have insulated himself psychologically from the shortcomings of the camp.

"Didn't you say something about the POWs and how they aren't treated like they should be?" Annette's words were the first she'd uttered since the conversation began.

"If you're standing on the gate, anyone who comes in, you're supposed to search. Any unauthorized items are not allowed in there."

"Yeah, but aren't they supposed to be given proper food and medical care?"

"Sure, they're supposed to, but they don't get it."

"But under the Geneva whatchamacallit, you're supposed to," Annette insisted.

"But look here, the United States signed the Geneva Convention, but Hanoi and Saigon didn't sign that thing. So they give you a Geneva Convention card, and them people aren't going to honor that card if they didn't sign it. They're not part of it. That only make sense."

"But still ... the Americans shouldn't be helping with something that they——"

"Well, the Americans don't have that much to do with it, Annette. They got a few people there to search the stuff, but the POW camp is mostly run by the Vietnamese."

"But they shouldn't be there at all, if it's not run properly. Under the Geneva Convention——"

Their dialogue had an edge to it. John looked at me to confirm Annette's stupidity whenever she talked, and he appeared irritated when she did speak. It was a relationship that was to change toward the end of the week, when it became clear to John that I was interested in what Annette had to say.

The depravity of Saigon ensnarled John quickly. One week into his tour in the city, a Vietnamese taxi driver asked him if he wanted to make some money on the black market; 85 percent of the GIs in Saigon did, he said. A month later he got involved, buying radios and later refrigerators—"small stuff"—in the PX and selling them for double the price.

"The papa-san I was working for wanted me to rip off a jeep. I said, 'Well, I don't know about that. That's a little steep.' He said, 'We have nice major workin for us. I introduce you to him tonight.' So we went down to Maxim's, a big Vietnamese nightclub. This major was in the combat engineers and was ripping off generators and transformers. He tried to convince me that there was big money in it. Claimed he was sending home $4000 a day . . . a day! Well, I never did work up enough nerve to rip off a jeep."

Yet John had not brought home any money from Vietnam. He was not one to plan ahead. He had dabbled in the black market only before he knew he was going on R&R. "I went downtown, done my thing, and split," he said. His thing before an R&R constituted making $1200–$1500, and it was all gone when he returned in seven days.

John Herndon had three R&Rs, one more than regulations allowed for fifteen months in the country. He accomplished that by the ever-present "friend in personnel"— a crucial factor in his desertion later. Hong Kong was a hassle, he said: "Just like Saigon without the shooting. Everybody's after your money." Australia was "terrific." He was the only buck sergeant on the first R&R flight to Sydney. "You never saw so many women in your life as there was at that airport. You could take your pick. I went with a girl who took me out to her parents' house right outside of Sydney. I spent seven beautiful days in Australia and loved every minute of it." And in Hawaii, he was treated to escape, American style.

"I had a room in the Waikiki Grand Hotel," he said, "and went to all the nice nightclubs. Just having a good time . . . getting really drunk . . . going around with expensive women. They're not hard to find in Hawaii. They're set up. You'd be surprised how they're set up: $30 a half an hour, $60 an hour, and $150 all night."

But the incident John remembers best from that vacation in Hawaii went as follows: "Me and another guy ran out of cigarettes so we walked into this country club right off the beach. A guy comes up and says, 'What're you doing here?' and I said, 'Just trying to get some cigarettes.' And he said, 'We don't sell cigarettes to people like you.' And I said, 'What the hell're you talkin about?' And then this black man comes over. I had this Vietnam jacket on, see, and he says, 'What's the matter, boys?' I explained, and he invited us into the club, put us in front row tables. Bought us dinner and drinks. I thought he looked familiar, but I couldn't place him. Then he left us, and the show started, and the announcer introduced Sammy Davis, Jr., and out comes this same guy. I almost fell out of my chair. He was playing there. Anyway, he took us to his apartment. He pays $2000 a week for that thing up on Point Diamond Head. He was terrific."

Toward the end of his week in Hawaii, John ran out of money and called his folks asking them to send him $300. His mother wired him $100. She said to me later, "$300 seemed like too much for him to spend in just one week."

Back in Vietnam the procedure for escape was strictly businesslike.

"You go in a bar, and you pay one hundred piasters for Saigon tea—one dollar. You tell a girl you'd like to go home with her. It'd cost you three hundred piasters. So you give the bar owner three hundred piasters. You go home with the girl to her house, you ball her, and you come back."

John had some appreciation for how American involvement had contributed to this system.

"When I went over there," he said, "you used to have to pay one thousand piasters a night for a hotel. At that time, one thousand piasters was ten dollars. Now five hundred piasters is one dollar .... These poor dirt farmers out in the rice paddies—they used to make one hundred piasters, two hundred piasters a month, which was enough to live on. Then the Americans came over, and the peasant found that this was not enough to live on anymore. Therefore, the young women turned to prostitution to try to support the family."

John had also taken a three-day R&R in Vung Tau where

"the Americans and the Viet Cong take R&R together." He knew this, he said, because he had met the enemy there. There had been a drunken argument over a girl. "This Vietnamese guy comes up and says, 'Hey, that's my girl.' I felt the girls were all open. They were all prostitutes anyway. Anyhow, we had this argument, half joking. He said he would blow me away, and I said he better sit down before I knocked him down. He asked me if I were for the war or against it. I said, I was against it, but 'if you don't shut up, I'm going to make war right here.' He said he was with the NLF, and I said, 'Well, good for you.' We sat down and started talking. He showed me his identification. But unfortunately I didn't make any dear friends who wouldn't shoot me once I got out in the field. Fun and games for three days and then you go out and shoot each other."

In October 1967, John Herndon got in his first serious trouble with the military authorities. The incident is a classic of the Vietnam war. He was charged with being AWOL and with shooting a Vietnamese girl. John described it like this:

"I'd gotten stuck in front of a BOQ when this little battle broke out. It was harassing fire from the enemy. They'd gotten a sniper in a hotel across from the BOQ. He had an automatic weapon. I was walking out the gate when the sniper opened up. The Vietnamese guard there had dropped down because he was scared. So when the shooting started, I jumped in the bunker where the guard had the machine gun, and I opened up at the hotel across the street, 'cause that's where the fire came from. And this little Vietnamese girl got shook up; she panicked, and she ran in between the crossfire and got killed. Some MP ran out, found her identification, ripped it up, and then listed her as a 'confirmed kill,' a VC kill, because she didn't have no identification.... Tearing up IDs was the main way we got our body count of 'confirmed kills' during the Tet offensive later. But anyway, it didn't work that time. I got blamed for her death. I felt bad about it, because she was only eight or ten years old, even though it's a toss-up as to who shot her—him or me.

"Anyway, they jammed me in LBJ [Long Binh Jail] and left me for forty days' pretrial confinement. The Vietnamese were pressing the charges pretty hard. At least that's what I gathered. They didn't let me know too much. Anyhow, they dismissed the charges later at a court-martial because they couldn't pin 'em on me."

In January 1968, with fourteen months of Vietnam duty behind him, John prepared to go home. He processed out, and on January 25, 1968, went to Tan-Son Nhuet Air Base to catch a plane home. He lounged around the airport, waiting to board, when suddenly there was a tremendous explosion. A 122 Russian rocket had smashed through the roof of the airport. The GIs scattered. More rockets came in, but the first had wounded twenty-one and killed one. The cataclysm of the Tet offensive had begun. John rushed to the headquarters compound. "There was nothing else to do," he said. There he was issued a weapon; he was the only combat qualified soldier in the compound at that time. From there he was assigned back to his MP unit and was in continuous combat for the next five days. In looking back on the airport crisis, when the first rocket hit, John remembers saying,

"What the fuck is this? A man's trying to go home, and they're still trying to kill him."

On January 31, John was on Highway 1 in Saigon. Rockets were raining down all around and one slammed into a two-and-a-half ton truck full of MPs. Twenty men were killed instantly. Two lay wounded under the truck. John was with a team trying to save the two when another rocket exploded in front of him, a fragment slicing across his left cheek and ear and another embedding in his chest. He was taken to a hospital outside Bien Hoa and sewn up.

In the hospital, John Herndon was presented with the Army Commendation Medal. The citation read:

Through his untiring efforts and professional ability during a coordinated Viet Cong attack throughout the city of Saigon, Republic of Vietnam, he consistently volunteered his services and contributed to the outstanding manner in which the United States Army Head-

quarters Area Command was able to accomplish its
mission. Despite sniper fire, mortar, and B-40 rocket
rounds, he assisted materially in the feeding, housing,
resupply, and maintenance of security for more than
35,000 American military and civilian personnel stationed
in the city of Saigon.

His commendable performance and devotion to duty
have been in the highest tradition of the United States
Army and reflect great credit upon himself, his unit, and
the United States Army.

On the night of February 4 he was taken to the airfield
at Bien Hoa with patches on his face and chest and put on
a C-141 jet transport. No commercial planes were flying out
of Vietnam during the Tet offensive. John sat between two
WACs. The plane taxied to the end of the runway. As it
lunged forward tracer bullets flashed from the side of the
runway and one of the WACs passed out. "As the plane
took flight," John said, "you could hear everyone in the
plane sigh. We made 'er. We're goin' home!"

John David Herndon was going home with the physical
and psychological wounds of the war upon him.

"I was just reading here in the newspaper about a woman
who got hurt in an avalanche. When I hear about things
like that I won't cry, but my eyes will water. It's like I
want to. It's been that way ever since I come back from
Vietnam. Anybody who gets hurt . . . it's like I feel it myself. It's really kind of hard to explain."

Annette had wanted to go to the fireworks display on
Bastille Day the year before, but John had refused to accompany her.

We'd been talking in their apartment for several hours;
it was getting to be 8:30. I invited them out to dinner. It
was an instinct that I was to have throughout the week—
that I wanted to feed these two. They looked like they
needed it. The combination of the dried noodles on the
table and the package of sandwich ham that Annette slipped
out onto the porch to keep it cool and away from the cat

confirmed the need. But also I did not know what food John would be getting in the week that was to follow, and conceivably the five years after that.

There was no café close by, so we walked to the Place d'Italie some twenty minutes away. Along the way John told the story of the time on Place d'Italie when an English girl was being raped by a Frenchman and a number of Frenchmen simply stood around and stared. The girl was screaming, but no one called the police.

Annette cracked, "Everybody knew there was no point in calling the police. They'd just arrive an hour later, take the name of the girl, and the fact that she'd been raped."

John had hit the Frenchman in the back of the skull with his knuckles, and it had stunned the man enough to allow the girl to escape.

We sat down in the café, and John said, "You see that little lady over there?" I looked over to a leathery, middle-aged woman sitting alone in the corner.

"She's an American. She was married to a policeman at the Prefecture and renounced her American citizenship. He died, and she hasn't had much money since. I figured she'd be coming over here for a few francs, but it looks like she got it settled.... She helped me out a little at first, gave me a few addresses that were helpful. I'd go ahead and give her five francs if she'd been in trouble."

They ordered the cheapest steak, at eight francs, as did I. The waiter grimaced and tried to force hors d'oeuvres and wine on us. He was generally unpleasant, appearing to find it distasteful to wait on such unelegant customers, so I made a point of pestering him for matches, or water, or anything else I could think of. John and Annette loved it. They had ceased to fight back at this French nastiness themselves.

Meanwhile, John continued his tale.

He was taken to Walter Reed Hospital where plastic surgery was done on his ear lobe. "They did a beautiful job," he said. After a leave home, he was assigned to Fort Jackson, South Carolina, where the doctors were overjoyed that he had feeling in his ear. At Fort Jackson he began the dull life of a stateside soldier. Adjustment to the slow pace was something of a problem. "It was strange. The beds was too soft. The food was too rich. I was used to getting only fifteen to twenty minutes sleep at a time. I couldn't sleep for two hours straight. I walked around all tensed up, waiting for something to happen. I just knew something was going to happen."

He was placed in a training unit where he took a light vehicles driver's course and a heavy vehicles mechanic's course. GI life proceeded normally until one day, driving to work from his off-post apartment, he had a bad automobile accident. His arms and legs were badly hurt, and his Vietnam face wound was opened up again. He spent two months in the Fort Jackson Hospital. When he felt himself recovered, he found that he could not get a release. This was a story I well understood, for I too had once been in the Fort Jackson Hospital—except with a cold. The rule was that one could not get out until one's temperature dropped below 100. They fed me endless aspirins in a ward of forty coughing recruits, but the temperature would not drop. I was convinced I'd catch pneumonia if I stayed. Finally, to get my release, I put the thermometer in cold water. But John had no such escape. On September 13, 1968, he sneaked out of the hospital and went home to Baltimore—his first AWOL. He stayed for a month. After the Army called his home, he reported back, but to Fort Meade, Md., rather than Fort Jackson. In a summary court martial, he was reduced from sergeant to corporal and restricted to the company area for thirty days.

In December 1968, upon his release from restriction to post, John married the sister of a GI friend in the Towson, Md., courthouse. He'd met her several months before on a leave from Fort Jackson. They were to have one month of marriage together—"not even enough time to get used to one another," John said—before, in January 1969, he received orders to Germany for the 509th Infantry Airborne Mechanized Brigade. John was confused and hurt. He went to see a major about it. He said he didn't want to go to Germany. He'd just gotten married. The Major replied, "Well, son, you have to go." And he did.

The 509th was a spit-and-polish elite unit that is the European counterpart of the 101st Airborne Brigade. The Pentagon described the unit to me later as a unique force within the European Command, because of its dual mission of being airborne as well as infantry. It has, therefore, a high priority on personnel, they said, and is never under strength, and has a higher percentage of officers and noncoms per soldier than other European units. The barracks are better; the welfare benefits more extensive; the morale higher, with the added benefit, according to the Pentagon, of exotic trips throughout Europe for maneuvers. In the six months John was with the unit, he made airborne jumps in Greece, Spain, Luxembourg, Italy, Belgium, England, Norway, North Africa, and Portugal. It was after one such exotic trip—to Greece for three days of jumps—that John was to desert for good.

The act of desertion is, of course, an act of some significance. It can be punishable by death from a firing squad, as in the case of Private Eddie Slovik in World War II. It is often linked with treason, but then what is the meaning of treason when it is committed against the country which is the greatest purveyor of violence in the world today? It is normally associated with cowardice, but John Herndon is obviously no coward. Its dictionary meaning is "to leave in a lurch," but the American Army is clearly doing quite well without John. It is frequently assumed to be the product of bad advice or poor company, but John's act was totally his own. So the old-liner is left with the explanation that the Army chose later: that John was just a rotten egg.

Before I ever met John Herndon, my presupposition about the act of desertion—committed by 100,000 American soldiers in 1971—was that it flowed from gut reaction, seldom intellectualized, and then only well after the act itself. The act first; the leap of faith, the arguments later. I knew that when I was a soldier I had intellectualized the process of revolt; my escape was to write a novel about the dilemma, considering the options through a fictional character and letting him get the ax in the end, not me. As the Spanish proverb goes, "Paper bleeds little." I had been "honorably" discharged. The emotion had been there, but not the will to act.

Six months after John arrived in Germany, he learned through a friend—the ubiquitous "friend in personnel"—that he was again on levy for Vietnam.

"After spending a certain amount of time in Vietnam, you know how things are run there. You wish not to go back, that's it. You don't like the way things are going. When they told me I was going back, the first thought that entered my mind was 'Oh no I'm not.' Why did that thought enter my mind? It wasn't because I thought I was going to get killed over there, because I'd already been in combat. I wasn't worried about that. I would have gone back to Vietnam—voluntarily—if there was some way I could help the people without killing the people. And seeing that there was no way I could help them without killing them, not in this war anyhow, why should I go back?

"So when they said you're going back, I said to myself, 'Oh, I have a choice now. I can either go to Vietnam or I can go someplace else.'" John was to say cryptically in an interview with *The New York Post* a month later: "They told me to go back to Vietnam or go to the stockade. So I went to France."

But that was John Herndon, the public figure, talking. The decision had been more agonizing, slower in coming than that.

"I knew I didn't want to go back to Vietnam. Because I was against the war to begin with. I didn't like the techniques that the American military was using over there, the way they were going about it. That was definite. I was not going. The choice was where *do* I go now. You've got to find a place. You just can't run off and have nowhere to go.

"'This is Europe.' I said to myself. 'I could go to Sweden. Now Sweden's a long way, 'cause you have to go through Norway and there's a chance of getting caught. France is the closest.' And that's when the thought first occurred to me.

"In Germany there was a friend of mine who was in my unit. He'd just spent eighteen months in Paris. He'd come back, and he got a year's suspended sentence. I was talking to him and told him I thought I might like to make the trip. He had a few friends. He gave me a couple of addresses. 'Get in touch with them,' he said, 'and they'll give you a place to stay.' " (Unfortunately, these contacts were not in Paris.) "I did make contact with them though—and they gave me a place to stay, and gave me names of other people who could help."

Had the thought of desertion ever occurred to him in Vietnam? I asked.

"Going AWOL, perhaps, not actually the thought of desertion when you're over there, you kind of wonder, where am I going to go, what am I going to do, how am I going to get out of this country? If you're to do something like that, you gotta plan ahead, know exactly what you're going to do, keep your mouth shut, and make your move."

Had he ever seen any anti-war literature in Germany? No, was the answer. Had anyone ever urged him to desert? No. So the decision was completely internal? Yes. Indeed, the privateness of John's personality, the product partly of his upbringing, partly of his military training, but mostly of his exile's cunning that had enabled him to survive in that predicament so long, was a problem for us then. He wanted to tell me his story, and yet . . .

"I've got so much to say that's bottled up inside of me," he said as we came to the close of this first five-hour talk. "I'd really like to get rid of it. Sometimes I feel like I want to cry when I can't say what I really want to say."

★ WEDNESDAY, MARCH 15, 1972 ★

I'd come home from the Place d'Italie the night before tremendously excited. John was, I thought, exactly right for this first, all-important test case on amnesty. He had endured the worst aspects of an immoral war in his own flesh. He was representative of the kind of Americans whom the country has forced to fight the combat of the war. He had deserted not because of what he had heard about the war, but because of what he knew of it, and his act had been his own. This was no "victim of bad advice," no rear-echelon spoilsport.

But most important to me, his decision to return openly, to face the charge of desertion in military court, to risk five years at hard labor if the Army chose to make an example of him, was his own choice. He was not being manipulated into it.

At 11 A.M. Mike Uhl came to my hotel room with John, and the first strategy meeting of the week took place. They believed that they *could* move quickly, Mike said. When? Friday? Over the weekend? They hadn't decided yet.

The scenario Mike described combined strict secrecy and brazen openness. The plan was to go directly to the airport with John's plane ticket in hand and demand that he be boarded solely on the strength of his military identification —"John is going home to answer charges of desertion, and what do you mean he can't do this?" One key to this strategy was surprise. The U.S. Embassy should not know until the last minute what was happening, lest they make a deal with the French authorities. Mike doubted that the French would care what happened. "They should be glad to get rid of one more 'barnacle,' " he said. John took no offense at this remark. The airline's only concern would be the ticket. If in the end John should not be boarded, it should be clear that the Americans bore full responsibility. The lines for a test case on amnesty had to be drawn clearly between the refugee and his *own* government.

Why was it so essential to confront the American authorities in Europe when the real confrontation over amnesty would come in the States? I wanted to know. Might not the Embassy simply accede and give John the necessary documentation to get him legally to the States for his surrender?

Mike explained that there were two reasons. "First, the normal procedure in the case of AWOLs is to send the soldier back to his unit. That would mean Germany for John, which would defeat the whole purpose of the operation. Second, we are not playing this on the Embassy's terms. Those terms mean no statements at the airport, a military police escort, a deserter under wraps. Safe Return is sponsoring this action, not the war establishment." Mike reminded me of the significance of John's case: that he was the first deserter to return home openly, to fight charges of desertion. Two thousand or so deserters who had returned before him had simply given themselves up, creating the impression that they couldn't take exile from America any longer and were willing to accept whatever punishment the military establishment meted out.

The uncompromising stance of the operation appealed to me immensely. I only questioned how we were to elevate John's case above the bureaucratic level of airport immigration clerk to the political level. His fate had to be a high-level decision either in the American Embassy or the French Ministry of the Interior to be an effective political act. This was to be worked out later.

The other key to the strategy was press coverage. In the months that preceded the March trip to Paris, Mike and Tod had talked a good deal about this factor. Coverage of the test case was vital to political impact obviously; but it also provided a certain insulation against police and bureaucratic action. Mike and Tod had interested Steve Young of CBS Television in filming the return. Steve was enthusiastic about the story and had proclaimed his willingness to fly over to Paris on twenty-four-hours' notice to film the boarding, and actually to accompany the deserter on the plane to New York. Thus, the presence of TV cameras at the airport would insure that if John were refused passage, it would be made clear that the Embassy was responsible. If he were refused, John and the whole entourage would go there immediately for an explanation.

Mike and Tod had weighed and rejected the option of phony leave orders as a method of getting John boarded. This technique, often used by deserters moving between countries which offer political asylum, would only add to military charges that might be leveled against John and would detract attention from amnesty. Other questions of strategy remained to be worked out. Safe Return preferred to bring John into Washington's Dulles Airport, (1) so that he would be assigned to Fort Meade, close to his home in Baltimore, where his Congressman, Perren Mitchell, whose sympathy with amnesty was already known, could exert an influence, and (2) because of the story's impact on the nation's capital. However, the possibility of going through Canada remained open.

And so John and I walked off for lunch, our heads swimming with the promise of reentry within the week, the doubts and fears not yet entering our thoughts. John wanted to take me to an Algerian restaurant on the Left Bank near Notre Dame, where you could get couscous for five francs.

"When I first came here, I didn't have much money... and I had to find places to eat, like this North African place," he said. "I could come here and get a meal for five francs. Anyplace else I'd go and get the same meal, it'd cost ten francs. You have to learn to conserve your money. Americans have a wild way of spending money, especially if they're in Paris. So in order to make your money last, you've got to go to cheap places to eat."

As we searched the narrow byways off the Quai de la Tournelle, I asked John if he liked the strategy of surprise. He did, but I sensed that he felt isolated from the planning. He placed more faith in Tod than Mike, probably because he had spent more time with Tod in the past, though he had not seen much of him since we had come to Paris. I told John that I'd make sure he had a long talk with Tod the next day.

We finally turned down a small street called Rue Maître Albert, passing some man standing in a corner with his back to us, and entered a boisterous, nameless café. The waiter threw up his hands in recognition of John. We were seated, John ordered, and we were soon brought wine in a plastic bottle, the semolina, and a piece of gristly meat swimming in a weak vegetable soup.

We were to talk above the slaps on backs and the loud jokes of the dingy North African bistro about John's life in exile.

Two years before in August, John and a buddy had been sitting in a bar in Mainz; after a few drinks, John had said,
  "Well, I'm goin'."
  "Where you goin'?"
  "I'm goin' to France."

"God, man . . . can I come with ya?"

"Sure, come on."

Twenty-four hours later, they were in Paris. This was the first of two "self-retirements" for John. His friend limped back to the unit in Germany in less than three weeks. But John was to stay in France from August 1969, to April 1970. He returned to the 509th Brigade in April 1970 on American Embassy orders for one reason: to clear up the paperwork for divorce of his wife of one month. There had been a terse correspondence between them when he had arrived in Paris. He wrote her of his desertion and asked her to join him.

She replied: "You deserted me. You deserted the Army. I want a divorce." John remembers sitting down on a bed and saying to himself, "Wow, man, what the hell is this world comin' to? A man does something and his own wife won't even back him."

He answered: You got a lot to learn yet."

She pleaded again: "Set me free. I'd like to be on my own. I'd like to have a divorce."

He answered: "Keep thinkin' that way baby, 'cause you file for it, and I'll sign it." That matter has never been cleared up. John heard through his parents that his wife had written to the Pentagon, telling them where John was, and asking them to pick him up. Her allotment checks had ceased after he deserted.

The two GIs had spent five days in Paris, sleeping in *métro* stations. They had a vague notion that they must find an organization that would help them. They knew two names: S.D.S. (Students for a Democratic Society) and A.D.C. (American Deserters Committee). John was to find out only many months later that by the time he arrived in Paris, A.D.C. had moved to Sweden, and S.D.S. had moved to Germany. Without skills, without contacts, without language in a very foreign land, John was operating on blind instinct.

The two walked about the streets of Paris, staying mainly around Place d'Italie and Place Pigalle, asking hippies if they knew of the organizations that they sought, avoiding the police as much as possible, bumming meals where they could. John had five dollars in his pocket.

"With all the fruit and stuff lying around, it was pretty easy to get something to eat. If you got near a church, you'd go in and try to explain your situation as best you could in English, and hope they understood. They'd always give you something to eat. I made a lot of friends among the bums. They used to give me food and cigarettes. They'd been there so long, they had their contacts. They knew where to get things at night. I had one friend who used to take me into a café at a certain time at night where he got free drinks. The owner was sympathetic. I went in there with him, and the owner gave me a drink, a pack of cigarettes, and a sandwich."

But after five days without making any contact, John's companion started talking about returning to their unit in Germany. John would have none of it.

"I figured I would find something eventually. If I'd of gone back in a few days or weeks, I would have been defeating my purpose. Why should I have left to begin with if I only wanted a vacation? I had a reason. I was against the war. They were trying to send me back to it, and I was protesting. . . . I didn't know where to start. I knew what I was looking for, but I didn't know how to go about it. But I wasn't going back. There was no way I was going to go to jail for doing what I thought was right. At that point I woulda starved to death before I went back."

And so John said to his buddy, "I don't know about you, but I'm going to the coast."

"You can't leave me, man," the friend replied. "I don't know the language. I don't have any money."

John gave him $2.50 and took off for the coast. For some reason he believed he might find a relief organization there. In Le Havre he ended up in a convent for two weeks, looking for help during the day, but finding nothing.

"You have to be at that convent at a certain time to eat," he told me. "If you're not there, you miss it. At a certain time every night the door closes. If you're not there, well, you're stuck out all night. I got caught with the door closed on me one night, so I started hitchhiking back to Paris."

It was his first stroke of luck. The following morning, outside the cathedral town of Rouen, he was picked up by a young man he was to know later as Luc Cloche.

"The guy was talking a lot about Yugoslavia and about Czechoslovakia. And after a bit, it seemed very obvious that he was a Communist, so I took a chance. I looked at him and said, 'I'm an American military man. I'm AWOL.' He jammed on the brakes in the middle of the Auto Route, and threw his arm over across the seat, and I said to myself, 'Holy Jack, he's going to kick me out on the highway.' He said, 'What can I do for you? How can I help you? Where can I take you?' I almost fell out into the road. It blew my mind.

"So I explained the situation to him. He was a Communist, see, but he took me to a fascist for help, a friend of his, and the fascist said, 'There's one man who can help you,' and he took me to a Socialist in the little city of Rouen." (Did John really understand these terms? I wondered.) "At that time I did not speak French, and they did not speak English. The Communist did, but he was the only one. The person I went to in Rouen made a telephone call to a woman, who was a professor of English there in Rouen at the university, and she translated for us."

Finally, after more phone calls, they told him that they had found an organization in Paris that would help. He stayed in Rouen for several days—the people there were to give him the greatest support and were to be the warmest human contact he was to find during his stay in France.

"These people knew me for about six hours. They laid a 500-franc bill, which is approximately $100, on the table, and told me I knew where the stove was, where the record player and the radio were. If I needed anything to eat, go buy it. I wanted to go to the café? Go, you got the money. Do whatever you want with the money.

"I was interested in an organization. Money didn't even interest me. I didn't have any, but it didn't interest me. I took the money, and put it in the cookie jar. I scrounged around the house, found some eggs and some noodles to eat. The next day, the Socialist said, 'Look, my sister will come and get you and take you to where I work, and then I'll take you to Paris in the car.' So at five o'clock she came and·we met him, and we started off to Paris.

"Well, about twenty kilometers outside Rouen, he said, 'Do you still have the 500 francs I gave you?' I said, no, I put it in the cookie jar. This guy, who don't speak much English, he looked at me and said, 'You stupid son-of-a-bitch,' and I said, 'Huh?' and he said, 'When somebody give you money, you don't put it in a cookie jar,' and he reached in his pocket and pulled out a 100-franc bill, about $20, and said, 'Now, you keep this. When you look for work, you gotta have some money.'

"So I kept his 100-franc bill. I got all settled down nice. I'd been working for two weeks, and I said to myself, I'd like to see this man again and thank him, give him back his 100 francs and let him know I was doing O.K. I believe in keeping up contacts. So I went back to Rouen to give him his money. He wouldn't take it. So I put it in the cookie jar and left and came back. We've been corresponding on and off."

The organization in Paris turned out to be the Quaker Center, presided over by an Englishman by the name of Tony Clay. Tony became something of a father figure for John Herndon during his two-and-a-half years in exile—to John and to the deserter community in general. From John's descriptions of him, he was a saint. Tony Clay helped John, but not before John sustained an interrogation by a man called Max—"the mysterious Max," I came to call him, because his name and adventures were to surface a number of times during the week. There was something marvelously sinister sounding about the descriptions of Max: short, fat, talking GI slang with a heavy Austrian accent, he was a Viennese professor of geophysics, forty-four years old, and in Heidelberg when we were in Paris, working underground with a program of resistance in the Army which included, but was not limited to, desertion. He is political father to deserters if Tony Clay is the human father.

Max's interrogation of John was tough and thorough. John described it as tougher than anything the CIA could stage. And John, who would claim that he had conducted similar interrogations of *arrivées* later, accepted completely the need for it: to ferret out stool pigeons for the Army's

CID (Criminal Investigation Division) or the CIA. John's interrogation began:

Max: What's your father's name?

John: "What's it to you . . . ?"

Max (in Viennese English): "Shut the fuck up and tell me your father's name. . . ."

Max was the one, according to John, who would say to Tony, "I'll chance him," or "I don't want to mess with him."

"If he'd chance you, he'd give you some money, find you some work, and a place to stay. If you screwed up, that was it.

"Max is definitely politically orientated," John said. "There's no doubt about it. As soon as he walks into the room, he wants everybody to shut up. He has something to say. He's cool. Max impresses me. He makes me feel mellow . . . you know, good. I'd trust Max with anything in the world. I've heard a couple of other deserters say the same thing. He knows what he's doing, collects everybody's address. He has a way of making money, not for himself, but for the cause. Communicates with everybody. Keeps right up to date. If this guy don't impress you, nobody in the world is going to impress you. He doesn't organize out front. He's got other people that do it, but he sets it up. . . . This guy is terrific."

"What's his last name?" I asked.

"He don't put it out. . . . I can tell you what it is, but I don't know if you ought to print it."

John passed Max's interrogation, and the Quaker Center placed him outside of Paris near Chartres, in a Quaker conference center called Château de Charbonnières. The Château, with spires and turrets that seem right out of *Grimms' Fairy Tales*, is run by two families of Quakers involving three generations, and sometimes caters to as many as one hundred visitors. John is the only deserter who has ever worked there. In Chartres, John received his *carte de séjour*, the document authorizing the bearer to stay in France. It had to be renewed every three months.

"I was the first deserter to receive a *carte de séjour* in Chartres. When I first went down to the offices, they'd never seen a deserter before, and they refused to give me a *carte de séjour* because they thought they were doing something wrong. So I made a telephone call to Tony Clay, and he made a telephone call to the police, and the police wrote a letter out there, saying you'd better give it to that man. And the next day when I came down they had it all typed up, and handed it to me. They said, 'Oh, excuse us, we had to be a little careful. We didn't know exactly the stand the government takes on exiles like you."

In order to receive this residence permit, a person is required to state the reason for his request. John described his condition as: "A Vietnam veteran, opposed to the war in Vietnam. They tried to send me back, and I did not wish to go back."

For seven months the Château was his base. When he was there, he did odd jobs. His room and board were taken care of. It was pretty; the people were nice, and the food sumptuous. The Château routine began with a big breakfast, continued with tea at ten, lunch, tea at four, a good French supper, and a snack at 10 before bed. John's waistline grew to 36 inches. But he also had the freedom to travel and often did with other deserters whom he came to know in Paris. In the time of his first exile, he traveled to Denmark, Spain, Italy, Switzerland, Sweden, Holland, and Yugoslavia. For documentation he used his military ID, and for the countries of tighter control like Spain and Italy, he carried phony thirty-day leave forms to which he had access. "You just keep your mouth shut and play the tourist thing," John said, "It worked out nice."

But life at the Château was isolated and dull after a time, and his divorce could never be settled until he regained an official status with the American Government. So in April 1970, John called Tony Clay, thanked him for all his help, and said he was returning to the military. Tony replied that he hoped to see John back when everything was straightened out

The soldier arrived at his unit on April 14, 1970. On April 27 a special court-martial convened. Sergeant John David Herndon was sentenced to four months at hard labor; forfeit of $60 a month for six months; and a bad conduct discharge. He was sent forthwith to the Mannheim Stockade. Four months was to seem like an eternity. The stockade, packed with eight hundred inmates, was a racial powder keg.

In the time John was there, there were four race riots, and the cooks, who were inmates, made an attempt to poison the entire prison population by putting rat poison in the orange juice. Fortunately, the concoction was found out before the prisoners tasted it.

"When I was in the Mannheim Stockade, all the colored people called all the white people pigs. If you asked them what that meant, they would say a white person. Now you got white pigs and you got black pigs, white niggers and black niggers. The term pig and nigger is the same as far as I'm concerned. . . . To a certain extent I came out with a racial prejudice, not toward the black people in general, but toward the certain few I came in touch with. There's good and bad with every race. Unfortunately I was in with the bad. I disliked the ones I was with very, very much. . . . You had to stay on your toes all the time. Someone was always throwing a punch at you."

He complained that there was not enough food or medical care or recreational time. The doctor would come by daily and say "How do you feel?" and if a prisoner made a complaint the inevitable prescription was APC (aspirin) and cough syrup. In order to handle the racial problem, the authorities segregated blacks and whites during recreational times. "They had no right to do that," John said.

On August 6, Herndon was released from jail. His waistline had dropped from 36 inches when he left the Château to 29 inches when he left the stockade—in five months. At his unit he dutifully inquired up the chain of command about his bad conduct discharge. He was informed that the Board of Review had suspended it; that Major General Elmer H. Almquist, Jr., the convening authority, had refused to sign it; and that he was to return to duty. His first sergeant said further that due to the bad time he'd pulled in the Long Binh and Mannheim stockades, he had over a year of service left, and that he was headed back to Vietnam.

"I said, 'But I don't want to go back to Vietnam. I'm still opposed to the war,' and he said, 'It's not what you want; it's what your country wants.' And I said, 'O.K., fine . . . well, thank you,' and I came back to Paris."

He arrived in Paris August 16 and called Tony Clay. Tony said he had not expected to hear from John that soon, and what had happened? John replied, "The status is unchanged." He had come with a different buddy this time, who, like the first, went back after three weeks.

Exile for a refugee, ill-equipped with education or language or technical skills, is a never-ending battle for survival. For John Herndon, essentially Appalachian in temperament and outlook, the time from August 1970 to the gray evening that Tod Ensign and I arrived at his apartment in March 1972 was a scramble for a pittance to live on, being chased from one job to the next, struggling with the French language, contending with the ambivalent feeling among the French people and French bureaucracy toward desertion, socializing with French and American intellectuals and anti-war activists who would pick him up and drop him, descending into heavy drink and bumming, hitting bottom with a suicide attempt— all softened only slightly by his authoritarian relationship with Annette. As he would say in his airport statement, "Forced exile is a high enough price to pay. . . ." And yet it is a heroic story, proving the infinite resilience of a human being, inducing in John an overflowing generosity toward others who were down and out, avoiding the pitfall of drugs, developing a toughness which was to emerge in the ordeal of his return. John was to look back on his adjustment to exile as a considerable achievement, and it was in its own way.

He stayed only a short time in Paris, and then took off for the south of France to work in the fields during harvest. He was, in those first months, to pick grapes, olives, dates, and flowers. Who suggested such a thing to him?

"Nobody. I just took off down there. I mean, if you're going to find work, you got to look for it. You see, I was in Germany, and they had foreign labor picking grapes over there, and I figured it'd be the same thing here."

How would he go about getting hired, I asked.

"You just go to the City Council of any little town, and ask them for a list, and they give you the list of people who need help, because they use foreign labor. You average about thirty francs a day, room and board, and five liters of wine."

"They expect you to get drunk every night?"

"Some of 'em, yeah."

In one little town near the German border, John lived with a French wine-making family; picking their grapes by day, and spending his evenings in the local café with his fellow workers. It had been an international group with representation from Czechoslovakia, England, France, Brazil, and a girl from "Prague, Hungary." "We'd all get together at the café and talk and listen to music," he said. "We'd talk about the problems of the world and about resistance in the army . . . and what life was like in Hungary and Russia. It was a very quiet slow life. Everything almost comes to a standstill. It's not like Paris. I liked the country. It's O.K. for a couple of weeks, maybe a month. But then you just got to get back to the bright lights."

When the seasonal work expired, he returned to Paris. He worked at whatever odd jobs he could find: carpentry and welding were his mainstays. His two problems were the discrimination against deserters and his lack of papers.

"You could stick with some jobs. It depends upon the employer. Most employers find out you're an American deserter, they turn cold, say, 'Well, we can't use ya.' Another thing is that you have to have a *carte de travail* [working papers]. They're hard to obtain. Your employer has to pay 300 francs for you to get one. That's why the majority of the employers will not take a man without one. If he has one, they'll take him. . . . I've applied about four times for a *carte de travail,* and been refused. Been refused on the grounds that there are French people unemployed in that certain field, and I couldn't receive it. They've got a big unemployment rate here in France right now and there's a priority system for jobs. First come the former colonies of North Africa: Tunisia, Morocco, Algeria; then come the Portuguese; then the Italians; and when all these countries pass by, then come countries which don't have agreements with the French on labor, like the United States. Plus it's even harder here now, because they had a 20 percent cutback in farm labor not long ago.

"So every employer has to pay the 300 francs for the *carte de travail,* but it depends upon if you come over here from one of these countries with an agreement. He'll still pay the 300 francs, but the worker's guaranteed a job and his *carte de travail* before he comes. Another thing is that the employer normally takes it out of your pay. It's illegal, but they do it. It's a common practice. . . . Now, 300 francs is a lot of money, when you consider that the minimum wage is 800 francs [$167] a month, and also when you consider that if you go out and buy a suit here in Paris, it'll cost you a minimum of 500 francs. You pay your rent, and you starve for at least a half a month."

John's work record was marked by incessant fits and starts. At welding, which was his chief skill, he had made as much as $180 a week in the States. In France the highest salary he had ever been offered as a welder was 1250 francs a month ($260)—but he was canned three days after he was hired when the employer discovered his situation. At least he was paid for the three days. Another time, he had worked a month as a welder, when the employer found out he was a deserter, and canned him without pay. The employer kept no records, so there was no recourse. He worked at odd carpentry jobs when he could get them, never making above the minimum wage of 800 francs a month. His longest job was in a silk factory, La Soie de Paris, owned by a man called Levy, who was liberal and hired him *because* he was a deserter. The job was also at the minimum wage of $167 a month. (In America, his lowest salary had been $100 a week at a Baltmore paper factory.)

John worked at Levy's along with three other deserters for several months, until they were all fired in a dispute over the pilferage of scissors and ball-point pens. After a layoff of four months, Levy rehired John when one of the other deserters admitted the stealing. John was so grateful to be working again that he worked thirty-six hours straight in the first two days on the job. When he came home, Annette looked at him suspiciously. "Where you been?" she snapped at him. John told her he'd been at work.

"She thought I'd been out on a binge. But when she found out I'd started working again, she was so happy. She took my clothes off me. Put me between clean sheets. I was exhausted. She even called Levy to make sure it was true."

John worked another couple of months at Levy's until Levy had to lay people off because of financial difficulties. All in all, John had worked about six months out of the year.

"The only thing I knew was American standards of living. I come over here and get a job at 800 francs a month. Now, what's 800 francs a month? It's nothing, about $160 a month. You just can't go out here, like you did in the States. It just don't last. It may last to the seventh or eleventh of the month, or the fifteenth if you're lucky, and then you're broke. So you have to ask your boss for money to get to and from work . . . really, really scrimping at the end of the month. You can't go out to cafés and drink beer. You can't go out to restaurants. So you know it takes a long, long time to adapt to a pay-cut that vast.

"Actually, I really didn't adapt until I started living with Annette. Then I realized that I had to watch my money. There were two of us, not just one. There were things we wanted to do. Things we wanted to try to buy together. But we never had the money. Oh, we could make it O.K. though."

They began living together in the fall of 1970. They had met in the fall of 1970 at the home of another deserter, Jim Morrissey, where John was living at the time. After their first meeting, John went south on one of his seasonal jobs. When he returned to Paris, Annette began to appear at public functions where John was. They spent a night together, and in the morning she gave him a key to the apartment. "Don't forget to bring your bags when you come back," John remembers her saying.

Annette is an associate member of the Paris Quaker Chapter, and her Quaker pacifism drew her to the deserter community. "Deserters come to the Quaker Center," she was to say, "but very few come to Quaker meetings." She told me about the origins of her beliefs:

"I had one teacher in junior high school in Philadelphia. She was a very religious Protestant, kind of a fanatic. She would talk to us about different religious groups that we studied in history. I didn't like the common church. I'd been turned off as a kid. So I didn't go to church, but I was still believing. So we got on talking about wars and fighting and little battles that the settlers were having. The Mormons and all that bit. So she brought up the question: 'If there was a war, should we go off and fight?' Unanimous yes. Me too. I said yes. And then she said, 'But what if their religious beliefs don't lead them to fight, what then?' That's when it struck me—maybe nobody else got struck that way. However, I was perhaps the only one in the class that was interested in that kind of stuff. It probably would have come out later. Then finally after a while, through my history class, I got interested in Quakerism. So I wanted to go to Quaker meeting, but I was afraid to ask my mother. Finally I did, and she knew somebody who was going to meetings. My mother was glad that I was going somewhere.... So you see I've been a confirmed pacifist since I was twelve years old."

John was to say time and again how other deserters had either moved on to other countries or returned to their units, because of the difficulty of the language; and his own difficulties with language severely handicapped him. He insisted that he could get his point across in any discussion, and it was true that he could blurt out a phrase to be understood in a café or a grocery. But the fact was he never made an effort to learn French, and thus he could never integrate into French society.

Nonetheless, he had come into contact with a wide range of people, and his general feeling was that most were sympathetic to his act of desertion; that is to say, the people with whom he was naturally thrown together.

"When I was down south picking grapes, I'd go into a café. They'd find out you don't speak French, they want to know where you're from. 'I'm an American,' I'd say, and they'd say, 'What're you doing here?' They want to show you they remember the English they'd learned in school many, many years ago. They don't have much chance to practice it."

I asked him if he thought the French were anti-American.

"Not toward me and my situation, no, not at all. But toward the American Government or the American way of life, yes. 'American people get paid too much,' they'd say. But somebody in my situation opens them up. 'Course you always run into the bureaucrats, and the people who say, 'Well, I done this and that in Algeria, you know. What makes you any better than me?' Or, 'I went to Vietnam and I did my thing, and I left, now what makes you any better than me?' But when he finds out that I've been there, he says, 'Oh, that's a different story.' "

But John had to feel out most of the Frenchmen he met before he admitted he was a deserter.

"Before I make any statements, we set and we talk. Most people beat around the bush. The Vietnam War comes up, and if he's against it, I go ahead, ya see." The Vietnamese that he had encountered around the project where he lived had all approved of his situation. "Of course, they'd all been involved in the black market." John had some acquaintance with Portuguese deserters, of whom there are many in France, but had not discussed desertion with them. Annette commented, "They're so oppressed in Portugal that they don't say 'ouff,' and they don't say 'ouff' here either."

Through all of this, John had made his peculiar kind of adjustment—not integration, but existence. This was important to me, for part of the significance of John's return was that his exile was viable in its own way. And he was proud of its viability, proud that he had made it where others couldn't.

"I've learned so much since I've been here. . . . The new culture . . . the new way of life. It's an education. Now the military teaches you that if you leave the military to go someplace else, you'll never be able to survive. You come to a country where you do not know the language, and you can live here and survive here. O.K., it's a big achievement.

It's also an education. In fact, it's an opportunity. You figure if you haven't taken a foreign language in school, you can obtain it here. Therefore, whenever you decide to go back—a year, two years, six months, whatever—you can say, well, when I went to Paris, I learned something, I obtained something, and the time spent there, even if used as a resting place, is not lost."

For most deserters France is a way station. Few who come stay for very long. They either cannot take the life and go back to their units, or move on to Canada or Sweden. In March 1972, 122 American deserters were registered with the French police. (Pentagon figures show twenty-five living in France.) "Of course, there's more who aren't registered," John said. "Some of 'em have work. Some of 'em are pushing dope. One I know of's pushing other stuff—false passports.

"For most people who come over here, it's very difficult. They don't speak the language. And that makes it hard to integrate into the culture. The wages are not like the wages in America. And if you've got the habit of spending money like you do in America, the money just don't last. And that gets on their nerves. And also the fact that they haven't made up their minds what they're going to do. So France is more or less a resting point to gather yourself up and continue.

"There's an awful lot who come, stay three days and then go back after causing a lot of trouble for people who take them in. Everybody's broke their neck for them. . . . They come saying, 'Wow, Paris.' Big name. Big city. They've been away from home for some time. Maybe they've only spent a few months in Germany, not learning German, because most of the girls that you're tied up with speak English. Therefore, they figure France is the same way. If they haven't been to Vietnam where the girls don't speak English— well, the bar girls do, but not the other people—they're at a total loss."

"What percentage of those who stay in France end up pushing dope?" I asked him.

"People come here, they get work, and it's all gone in a week. Perhaps they've taken drugs in Germany. They have to find some means of living for two or three more weeks in a month. They say, 'If I can borrow so much money off this man, I can buy a kilo, break it down myself, sell it, and make me a profit, enough to buy another kilo, enough to pay him off.' And that's when they fall in debt. They do not want to, and will not, associate with American deserters because they owe this man or that a thousand. They're stuck in a pushing racket, because they make more, they think. Maybe they do good on the first kilo or two, more than they were making when they were working. So they quit their job, and they go into pushing and everything goes to rock bottom. It falls through. Therefore the only thing they can do is continue to push.

"Others take drugs over here and immediately they get snatched up and sent to prison. . . . Still others come over, they don't have any means of identification, don't have a *carte de séjour,* don't know if they can receive one, they pick up somebody's passport and the police pick them up for having a false passport."

I told John that many of the opponents of amnesty in the States were saying that the exiles who had fled the country or the service to avoid prosecution were criminals—rapists, murderers—and therefore should not be let back into the country. He said of the deserters he knew, only four had committed criminal offenses.

"The ones who come here have not had any type of criminal conviction in military life, or civilian life either. They've just got messed up over here in France; they didn't know they were allowed to stay here, so they had a false passport. They couldn't find a job, so they started dealing dope, and they got caught. It's not like these guys are bad. They all have their good points. They're not criminals. They're people running away, trying to find something, a little bit of home here away from home. Ninety percent of 'em want to go back, and they feel that it's the American people's responsibility to get them back."

I asked him about the deserter who sold false passports.

"Don't know how he operates—how he gets them. I know how he gets rid of them. He just sells them to people. I consider that his business, and not mine. Thataway, if I got tied up in something like that, the police would be looking at me, and it would jeopardize my position here. Would ruin everything I've been working for.

"And then, of course, there's Baby 1," John said. "He was the first deserter to come to France. He's been here since 1966 and has spent 90 percent of his time in prison. He's done everything imaginable. He stole a man's refrigerator once. The guy caught him, and he convinced the man he was taking the refrigerator out to repair it—with food in it and all. This man is so slick he could talk you out of the shirt on your back."

How many men had come for political or moral reasons? I asked. John thought. "About five," he said. "It depends on how you want to look at it. There was one man who left America right after he heard a VD lecture on Vietnam."

Annette had said: "I met one deserter down at the Quaker Center, and someone asked him, Did he leave the Army because he didn't want to get killed or because he was against the war? And he said, 'I've thought a lot about it, and I don't know.' But the fact is that he left for both reasons, because he didn't want to get killed for a no good war, and because he did feel it was immoral. If he knew he wouldn't get killed, would he have left? That he couldn't say."

How many of the men John knew had been in Vietnam? Three, including himself, was the answer.

We walked across the bridge over the Seine and onto the sand park under the shadow of Notre Dame. Children played on jungle gyms under the watchful eye of their nannies. Old men sat alone on park benches, their eyes shut, heads lifted to the sun. John told me that he had come here often when he was out of work and would sit and watch these same children and old people and wonder what he was going to do and what was going to become of him. We continued along the bank of the Seine, stopping once to look down at old men amid a crowd of children fishing with long bamboo poles. It seemed to me that I had seen a photograph of this once in muted blacks and whites. John said he had fished here too in his second exile, using a string and hook and bread for bait. "You catch what the French call 'gardons,'" he said. "They taste like mud." *Gardon,* I found out later, means "roach" in French.

I bade him farewell at the Métro St. Michel and went off to the Quai d'Orsai, where at the Foreign Ministry I obtained press credentials to attend the "Paris Peace Talks" the following morning.

When I returned to the hotel on the Rue des Écoles later that afternoon, Mike and Tod were back from CBS, and were chatting with John in a café up from the hotel. I joined them, with a quart of tomato juice because my head hurt from the Algerian wine.

They said some time had been lost in arguments at the plush Paris bureau of CBS as to whether the frizzy-haired cowboy and his portly hippie companion were authorized to use the phone to New York. But after some heated discussion, the secretary allowed it, and they made contact with Steve Young in New York. According to Mike, Young was CBS's man on the radical youth scene, but at the same time, he was new to the television side and thus did not pull so much weight. They informed Young that an operation was on for the weekend, and asked him if CBS was ready to cover the story. Young said he'd call them back the following night.

We talked of strategy somewhat, and it was decided that Monday would be the day, four days away. We could not be ready by the weekend, and the move would have to be on a business day. There was a piece of bad news along with this decision. There was no direct flight from Paris to Dulles International in Washington until June. The Dulles flight stopped in Boston, where the passengers disembarked to go through customs. Thus the choice was between Boston and New York.

It was then that John told us of his meeting with the military attaché of the U.S. Embassy two weeks before— on the same day that Tod's letter arrived proposing John's return. The story electrified us and made us realize in a flash what we were up against.

He had received in the morning of March 3 a bland summons from a "Captain Friedberg" asking him to come to the Embassy to discuss certain matters. "Bring along this letter," it had said. He went out of curiosity. He had nothing to fear, as his status in France was legal. He arrived, and "Captain Friedberg" asked him if he had brought the letter with him. John handed over the letter. "Friedberg" said he wanted to talk. John said, "Not in the Embassy." So they went to a nearby café. "Friedberg" ordered beer, and started asking about "weird things," according to John: questions about American deserters in general, about whether he knew any guys who were selling false passports, about the resistance movements within the Army. John had replied, "Look, man, I work fourteen hours a day; I come home and go to sleep."

According to John, "Freidberg" then said, "We know that James Reston, Jr., is going to be over here on such and such a date," and John had said, "Who?"

Another man joined them in the café. He was, John said, "CIA all the way." This man asked similar questions. John was noncommittal. And then the second man according to John, had said, "Look, man, all bullshit aside, I could give you a couple hundred francs beer money for the right answers."

The man reached in his pocket and pulled out 300 francs. John got up and said, "Fuck you." He walked out, terminating the interview.

In the afternoon mail, Tod's letter, dated February 24, arrived with four pieces of masking tape across the back. In it my name was mentioned, and the fact that I was considering doing a book making John the central figure. It was the second time John had heard of me.

Several weeks after our return to the States, I questioned the American Embassy in Paris about the buy-off attempt. The official version of the meeting between John and the military attaché was quite different. The Embassy asserted that John, not the attaché, had requested the meeting, and that if Herndon disputed that, he might produce a copy of the "alleged Embassy letter." Furthermore, the Embassy claimed that John, in a call to the Embassy, had offered "certain information": namely, the names and addresses of organizations assisting deserters around the world, in return for more money and a letter stating "he had performed a service." Finally, the Embassy stated the meeting broke up when the Embassy refused to provide any money for this "information."

I questioned John closely on this shocking reversal of his original account of the meeting. He vigorously denied the official version as a lie. Thus, one is left with two contradictory stories, and it becomes a matter of who, in 1972, one believes: his own government or his own friends. For Mike Uhl and myself, whose prejudices against official explanations are openly admitted, John's story rang true. We were inclined to believe that the Embassy version was a classic example of that infamous concept that we had both been taught as official doctrine in the Army Intelligence School at Fort Holabird, Md., and which so epitomized the Vietnam era: plausible denial. Plausible denial is the practice in embarrassing intelligence operations of always having an official denial available which rings of plausibility. The absence of the Embassy letter makes it a matter of John's word against the Embassy's.

From this point on, we assumed that the Embassy knew what we were up to and that we were being watched. The fear of a "parallel police effort"—a cooperative effort between the CIA and their French counterparts—was to grow and to provide exhausting tension during the next four days. But if they knew what we were up to, they did not know when it would come about.

The week had taken us all by surprise. Neither Tod nor Mike had expected that we would be making an attempt so soon. (Tod had intended at the start to spend a week on the Normandy coast.) So after John had left for Nationale, I proposed that we have our one *nuit de gala*. We went off to the Brasserie Bofinger, a two-star restaurant on the Rue de la Bastille, with polished brass rails and a decor of oak and gossamer curtains across the windows. It was a relaxed, joyous evening, our last. I had Oysters Marenne and Steak Bernaise, while the others had a medley of onion soup, snails, and sole. We drank a lot of wine from the Loire. I proposed that we maintain the "politics of joy" throughout the operation, not of Hubert Humphrey but of Daniel Cohn-Bendit. But it was a little phony. Mike often talks about the class nature of the deserter phenomenon—about how difficult it is for average Americans to accept desertion as a legitimate form of protest, especially if the deserter is inarticulate about the moral content of his act. And yet we were living that class dichotomy that night, for John and Annette were undoubtedly dining on the lunch meat that they had deferred eating the night before. But we are what we are, and we felt we were performing a useful task.

★ THURSDAY, MARCH 16, 1972 ★

When I had told Jon Randal of the *Washington Post* several days before that I wanted to attend the so-called Paris Peace Talks that week, he had seemed amused.

"I get a severe headache every Thursday when I go up there," was his comment.

But he had been a great help in getting me set up with credentials, starting with a call to the Embassy to ask if the "fun and games" were going on that week. Jon himself was happy to be liberated from the ordeal by Georges Pompidou's biannual press conference which would (mercifully) conflict that week.

The call to the Embassy was necessary, for the talks had been sporadic since early February. On February 10, Negotiator William Porter had canceled the meeting because of the meeting in Paris on February 11, 12, and 13 of the "World Assembly of Paris for Peace and Independence of the Vietnamese Peoples." Forty-eight French leftist organizations—political parties, labor unions, and citizens' groups—were sponsoring the event, and while some of these were Communist, the conference also attracted a good number of non-Communist peace groups, including the Quakers. Negotiator Porter said in his cancellation statement that the conference put "intolerable" pressure on the Allied negotiators and called the delegates a "horde of Communist-controlled agitators."

On February 17, the United States was still sulking and canceled again. On February 24 the meeting lasted seventeen minutes when the Communists, for the first time in the history of the talks, walked out. But instead of the "intolerable" pressure of a nearby peace conference, the Communist reason for cancelation was the pressure of a twenty-nine-hour air attack, February 17 and 18, on North Vietnam, involving 125 American planes. On March 2 and 9, the United States canceled the meetings, stating that the Communists had violated the procedural rules of the conference by walking out, and because of the "tone of statements" out of Hanoi criticizing Nixon's statements in Peking.

So it was on to March 16, the 146th Plenary Session of the four-sided talks which started January 25, 1969, after three months of negotiating on the shape of the table. The unmajestic Majestic Hotel, the site of the peace conference which is a block from the Arc de Triomphe, was built between the two World Wars. Its gray, unimposing cement face is in the bland style of government architecture. It was the Gestapo Headquarters during the Nazi occupation of Paris, and Eisenhower's headquarters after liberation. UNESCO was housed there in the fifties before it became the International Conference Center.

The routine at the Peace Talks always begins with statements to the press outside the building before the negotiators go in. I arrived in time for the South Vietnamese and North Vietnamese statements. Negotiator Pham Dang Lam of South Vietnam insisted that the Allied Eight-Point Plan was based on "logical, reasonable, and generous principles," and was "flexible enough to provide a solution to the war." If the Communist side would only stop demanding at the conference table what "they have not been able to achieve on the battlefield," he said, they could make progress. Several months later, with Quang Tri in enemy hands and Hue under siege, NVA Forces in Kontum, and Saigon jittery with the enemy at An Loc, with the last American combat troops withdrawn from the country, and no American official asserting that the South Vietnamese Army could back it without indefinite and sustained American air power, Lam's point had become mute.

Chief Negotiator Xuan Thuy of North Vietnam was "indisposed" that day (he has a convenient sinus condition), and his deputy, Nguyen Minh Vy, was there in his place. Vy looked a bit sleepy-eyed and thoroughly unemotional as his statement was read to the press by a translator. Presumably, the enemy's emotions are as dulled to it all as are the Allies':

It has been possible of late to witness a record performance by the Nixon Administration concerning its way of tricking public opinion about the Vietnamese problem. But the hypocritical words of peace and of good will will never be able to allow the escalation of criminal acts of war to be forgotten.

The American Administration has increased the air raids against the D.R.V. For eleven consecutive days, from the first to the eleventh of March 1972, American air power launched repeated raids against many regions, from the Vinhlinh zone to Nghean Province, killing and wounding many of the civilian population, for the most part women, children, and elderly persons. Even yesterday [March 15, 1972] these raids continued.

At the same time that it intensifies and extends the war over all of Indochina, the American Administration is adopting a more and more provocative attitude. It has put forward absurd pretexts for canceling several meetings of this conference while letting it be understood that it will continue to sabotage it.

Today we wish on the one hand to make these facts known and on the other to stress our just position.

The press then wandered back to the briefing room to await the opening statements. Luckily for me, the man from Group W Broadcasting had recorded Porter's statement, which I had missed, and we all huddled around as he replayed it:

Good morning, all. Glad to see you again. Well, we're back again, hopefully for more serious discussion than the kind they promised us last time. We'll be going over the substance of the problem with them. I'll give them a reading of the President's proclamation for Prisoner of War Week, which is a very powerful document, and we'll probe awhile on the prisoner problem itself, because of suspicion arising in the United States among the public that there's something very peculiar going on in those prisoner-of-war camps, in view of the adamant refusal of the North Vietnamese to permit an inspection of the prisoners by a neutral body as the Geneva Convention requires. We're not going to let go of that one obviously. See you later, perhaps.

The group hung on the words of the Negotiator, replaying the statement about "something very peculiar going on in those prisoner-of-war camps." They wanted to get it just right. Some historical moment, I thought.

Porter's opening statement was out on the desk in a half an hour. It began with customary condescension:

I do not intend to chide you excessively for the lack of courtesy you displayed here three weeks ago in walking out of the meeting. We have not had any illusions about that because over a long period you have regularly displayed a lack of good will in these talks. You did violate the rules of procedure, however; and if you deny having done so, then you are responsible for creating an interesting precedent. . . .

But the bulk of the statement was a recital of Nixon's Prisoner of War Week Proclamation of March 10 in which the President designated March 26–April 1, 1972, as National Week of Concern for Prisoners of War/Missing in Action. It hardly seemed a basis for negotiation. Porter ended his reading with the admonition: "On this issue you are arousing the just anger of the American people."

Where was Porter getting his reading of American sentiment on the prisoners-of-war issue? As fas as I knew, the coldest anger was coming from the families of the prisoners, who at a national convention seven weeks later adopted a resolution expressing "extreme distress" at the failure of the Nixon Administration to obtain the release of the prisoners. One of the wives, Mrs. James A. Mulligan, Jr., whose husband was shot down over North Vietnam six years ago, said she thought "disgust" was a better description of the conference's mood than "frustration."

"I think," she said, "it has become obvious to most of the wives of the known prisoners that we must either compel Nixon to end this war by negotiation or go out and actively support another candidate who will."

Porter's outburst of humanitarian rage about POW's also sounded a bit tinny in light of American bombs raining down on all of Indochina, and anyway, Red Cross inspection had never done anything about the tiger cages or the boxes of South Vietnamese POW camps. John Herndon could testify to that.

I was interested in the American "negotiating" position for its relation to the amnesty issue. Timing has always been crucial to the debate. Nixon's position was that the country could not consider amnesty until the war was over and the POWs were returned. Others attached the third contingency of an end to the draft with the institution of a volunteer army. On this basis the John Herndons might realistically bank their hopes for the first timorous amnesty sometime in 1974, when, barring unforeseen crises, the volunteer army went into effect—if Congress approved it.

I had argued in lectures that so long as the Vietnam effort could be supported by volunteers rather than draftees (which it could have been in March 1972 at the 100,000 mark, and at the 49,000 mark which Nixon made official in July 1972), and so long as we were in what, six months previously, the President had called a defensive posture in Vietnam, then the time was right to talk about amnesty. And what irritated me most was the pitting of one group of victims of the war against another. The U.S. Government could get the POWs back by negotiating an end to the war. It could also take up the amnesty question, the resolution of which was even more within its immediate power. But to refuse to negotiate the end of the war, and to use the POWs in North Vietnam as an excuse not to consider amnesty was and is a crude attempt at playing off one group of the Vietnam generation against another. *All* the victims of this war must be tended to immediately and equally, I had argued, if we are truly getting out of this admittedly mistaken war.

But Nguyen Minh Vy, that day in his reply to Porter, undermined Nixon's plea that we were in a defensive posture, and further charged that the United States was preparing to sabotage the Peace Talks—which of course the United States did the following week. Vy pointed out that, since the beginning of 1972, the United States had intensified its air attacks on North Vietnam, including the use of B–52s, by five times over the 1971 level of violence. He used United States figures on sorties to substantiate his claim, and said that these figures underestimated the true picture. He quoted a communique of his own from a North Vietnamese commission on U.S. war crimes:

> From the first to the tenth of March 1972, according to the first figures, American tactical air power made more than 300 sorties, dropping more than 550 explosive bombs, some hundred containers releasing thousands of gunshot bombs, fragmentation bombs, perforation bombs, and firing missiles, rockets, and bullets at 48 inhabited places in 37 communes of 9 districts of Vinhlinh, Quangbinh, Hatinh, and Nghean. These attacks resulted in 50 dead and 110 wounded, destroyed 70 houses, devastated vast areas of rice paddies, and decimated a large number of cattle. What is particularly serious is U.S. air power deliberately chose civilian targets like state farms, agricultural cooperatives, schools, stores, dispensaries, and Catholic churches.

These "grave acts," he said, were in "impudent violation of U.S. promises" in the bombing halt, "unmask the aggressive, warmongering, and obstinate nature of the Nixon Administration, and were "an insolent challenge" to world opinion. Vietnamization was "by nature radically opposed to the idea of serious negotiations."

I was catching Jon Randal's headache, so I left before the

NLF and the South Vietnamese could add to the verbiage. But at least we had the normal context for our little operation.

On the way back to the hotel, I read the *Herald Tribune*. Jack Anderson reported that Ambassador to France Arthur K. Watson got "gloriously drunk" on the flight to Washington for conferences with Nixon, kept shouting for more Scotch, grabbed the stewardesses, and tried to stuff $40 down their fronts. "He finally passed out, and witnesses reported that he appeared to be foaming at the mouth from white tablets he'd been chewing." Anderson also reported that Watson tried to recruit one stewardess as a mistress for his teenage son and threw grapes at her when she turned down the offer. We would hear more about this story later.

At the hotel we all rendezvoused at one o'clock. John had taken Tod to the Algerian restaurant at Rue Maître Albert. It was as if he was showing us all his side of Paris. John had been ebullient at lunch, asking what it was like in the States, and how had it changed in six years, talking nostalgically about his upbringing. Tod took this as an indication that John was already packed. He was psychologically prepared to go home.

Before lunch Mike and Tod had met with a French intellectual who was a long-time student of the French involvement in Indochina, author of a book on Dien Bien Phu, and a journalist for *Le Monde*. He confirmed Safe Return's thinking on several points. He concurred with the strategy of making no contact with the American Embassy until the day of the flight. He thought the political impact of the action would depend on our ability to dramatize the event. Everything must be planned so that the ultimate decision rested with the American Embassy and the airline. But how could the French be neutralized? Our journalist friend demurred at the suggestion that he personally be at the airport. It was not necessary, he said, and, furthermore, he was concerned about his own freedom to move in and out of the United States—which he thought such an involvement might jeopardize. But he gave Mike and Tod names of several people who could do as well or better at Orly. He was pessimistic about our chances of getting by the French authorities, and his pessimism had transferred to Mike and Tod. Both began to hedge their bets about whether we would board on Monday. Wednesday or Thursday of the following week as a departure date appeared more frequently in their conversation in the few days that followed the talk.

In the end, success would depend on security and the element of surprise. Still the French side worried me immensely. I had visions of never getting John beyond French immigration clerks, or not, at least, until the departure time of the plane had passed.

We now set the time of departure. It was to be TWA's Flight No. 803 for New York, departing Orly Airport at twelve noon Monday, March 28, 1972.

Later that afternoon Mike and I went off to see Maria Jolas in her apartment near St. Sulpice. The purpose of the talk was to give me an idea of the French experience with deserters from the beginning of the Vietnam era, and it was to be an exciting and useful talk on that. Maria Jolas, at the age of eighty a tall, fascinating, and commanding woman, was my only glimpse into the American expatriate life of Paris. Born in Louisville, she had gone to Berlin in 1913 to study singing under a leading German soprano. In 1919 she settled in. Paris. Maria and her husband Eugene had edited *Transition*, a small magazine that published Hemingway before *The Sun Also Rises* put him out of their reach in 1926, and James Joyce, for whom Eugene Jolas was later to become a secretary. They edited *Transition* from Colombey-les-Deux-Eglises, later the country house of Charles de-Gaulle. But now Maria is identified as much with radical causes as with her literary past. Her explanation of this involvement was: "Indignation is much better than cynicism . . . much more helpful."

She was incensed that day over the assignment of General John Donaldson, the "gook-hunter," as military attaché in Paris. Mike reminded her that he had served as Donaldson's S–2 in Vietnam. Maria then spoke of the letter that she and a group of American friends had written to *Le Monde* the day before about the matter.

le 15 mars 1972

Le Directeur
Le Journal "Le Monde"
3 rue des Italiens, Paris 9ᵉ
Monsieur le Directeur,

The recent assignment of General John Donaldson as military attaché at the U.S. Embassy in Paris has passed almost unnoticed. Yet, in the present context of the continuation of the war in Indochina, there is reason to find this assignment surprising.

Between November 1968 and January 1969, John Donaldson, a colonel at the time, is said to have fired several times from his helicopter on Vietnamese civilians, killing six of them. According to information furnished at the time of the charge made against him in June 1971, Colonel Donaldson is said to have found entertainment in engaging in automatic-rifle target practice on peasants in their fields.

Donaldson probably was given the benefit of a "non-suit" (the opposite would have been astounding, considering his rank and the public-relations disaster that the Calley trial had been). But many recent examples have taught us that "non-suit" does not always mean "innocence." As a matter of fact, the information published by *Le Monde* as well as by the American press leaves little doubt as to his guilt; and the charges brought by the pilot of his own helicopter have not been refuted.

Very closely associated with the henceforth famous acts of the Americal Division, of which he was named commander shortly after the Song-My massacre, formally accused by his peers of being a war criminal, General Donaldson finds himself shelved in . . . Paris! Would he be here as a Vietnam War specialist assigned to Ambassador Porter?

As American citizens, we the undersigned refuse to let slip past in silence this act of scorn which, according to us, is evidence not only of a great cynicism toward American opinion but also of a disturbing lack of consideration for French opinion.

Signée par: John Atherton, Luisa Calder,
               Jane Fonda, Susan George,
               Diana Johnstone, Maria Jolas,
               William Klein, Gabriel Kolko,
               Paul Lachance, David Jordan,
               Charles Sowerwine

I was astounded that one week in Paris could be such a microcosm of the Vietnam situation.

In a small sitting room Maria ensconced herself in a large chair by the window that opened onto the courtyard below, with children's voices amplified by the four walls. On the table by her were two sets of books: the collected papers of James Joyce and *The Pentagon Papers*. She was to captivate us for the next three hours, spinning endless stories with scarcely an interruption from us, and ending her paragraphs often with "*Bon!*" for emphasis.

During the years of the Vietnam escalation, Maria had been part of a group called PACS (Paris American Committee to Stop the War), which held a bimonthly *permanence*, meaning simply that at a certain time and place, with no promise of food or drink, people would come together for an expressed purpose. The purpose of PACS was to spread the word that the Vietnam War was immoral and had to be stopped. Someone came in once and quipped, "You haven't had much success, have you?" Maria told us parenthetically.

There is no doubt in Maria's mind that the 1966 decision to permit deserters political asylum in France was made by deGaulle himself. "Uncle Sam was pretty odious in France at that time," she said, "and deGaulle loved to tweak the nose of the American Government when he could."

In one of her fat dossiers on deserters, Maria confirmed this conclusion by this note: "The positive decision taken by the French Government seems to have come down from the 'directly political level' to the police level. It is now possible for all American deserters to legalize their position not only in Paris, but in all provincial prefectures, and without delay." This made France the first country in the world to provide asylum to deserters. Sweden came later, as did our other NATO allies of Denmark, Canada, and Holland.

The policy was not to be put to a test until several months later. On Christmas Eve, 1966, Maria Jolas got a call from a man who identified himself as an American deserter and asked for help. At that time, one had to be careful of the CIA, she said, and so she took the person's number and said she would call back in a half hour.

Maria had immediately phoned the board members of PACS. The Treasurer and Vice President of the organization and Maria put aside their celebrations ("I'm not at the age when I'm so sentimental about Christmas Eve anymore") and went to the outer ends of Paris to meet with the fellow. "We realized," she said, "that he was a poor thing, an *armes Ding*, as the Germans say. He was a social case rather than a political case. *Bon!*"

So the board had to decide what to do. Maria happened to have an old friend living in that section of Paris. Maria described her as a very "militant woman," one whose life had been spent in social work. She called the lady, and she agreed to take the deserter in. "Yes, we have a maid's room," she had said. "He can take his meals in the apartment, but warn him he must be discreet."

"Well, it turned out that he was most indiscreet," Maria said. "He wore his army jacket about everywhere, and he was mythomaniacal—the tall-story type."

This was Louis Armfield, a black soldier who was the first deserter in France. Peace groups took an interest in him, for he told a lurid tale of the job that he'd had in Vietnam, the unconscionable job of cleaning up and disposing of bodies after an American sweep through villages. A member of the *permanence* urged Armfield to write down his story. He did, and it was even more gruesome. The story was published thereafter in a British pacifist newspaper. Sometime after that, when Armfield had left the house of Maria's friend, he was picked up by the police as a vagrant when he was found sleeping in the back of a car on Saint Germain des Près. The story made the papers, and, in a dramatic move, Jean Paul Sartre and Alfred Kastler, a Nobel Laureate in physics, offered publicly to put up Armfield in their apartments if he could find no other place. And sometime after that it was discovered that Louis Armfield was an impostor, that he had never been in Vietnam.

Maria wrote me later: "He has been in and out of French jails ever since [drugs], an unconscionable liar, pimp, and what have you. I should add, however, that he arrived with a white boy who was immediately taken in hand by a very conscientious religious [Protestant] group in the Southwest. They got him a good job and surrounded him with friends and, when I last saw him two years ago, he had become incommunicado in English and could apparently only speak his own ungrammatical, mispronounced brand of fluent French. I was quite fascinated." Armfield was also the one whom John Herndon had found so "slick."

Louis Armfield became known as Baby 1, the term applied to him by the member of the *permanence* who had urged him to commit his Vietnam experiences to paper. This was none other than the mysterious Max. Thereafter, deserters were known to members of the sympathetic expatriate community numerically: Baby 2, Baby 3, etc. These first deserters to France were the "social cases" that Maria had talked about, the simple, uncosmopolitan, uncultured type to which PACS—and the French left in general—had great difficulty in relating. (Maria herself had been infuriated with John Herndon once when he showed up at a deserters' press conference in his jackboots, dungarees, and army field jacket: it was undignified.) But in 1967 the first political deserters began to arrive, men who were more open, less interested in hiding out, including Dick Perrin who had founded BOND, the first resistance newspaper at Fort Sill, Oklahoma; Andy Stapp, who later took over BOND and became secretary of the American Servicemen's Union; and Terry Klug, who later served a year in Leavenworth for desertion. And as the numbers of deserters increased and the political cases grew more numerous, PACS could no longer ignore the problem—or the opportunity.

Max had a special affinity for refugees. His own life had

been tragically dislocated by the Nazis. His parents, wealthy Jewish psychoanalysts, had fled to France from Vienna during the 1938 Anschluss. But in France his father could not find work, and it was decided that he and the ten-year-old child should go on to England. England however, was no more hospitable. Max's father was again unable to find work, and beyond that he was informed that not only would he not be able to bring his wife across the Channel, but he was himself about to be deported. He thereupon committed suicide, "a rather common solution of those days," according to Max. This was the first death in his family. Later, his grandmother was liquidated in Vienna, and his uncle was liquidated after being turned over to the Germans by the Vichy French. Miraculously, his mother slipped into Spain with a false Mexican visa and rejoined her child in New York in 1944.

So Max had seen Nazism in his own flesh, Maria said, and he knew the life of exile. On top of this he was a draft evader, having come to France after receiving a summons to the American Army during the Korean War. In the fifteen years he had lived in France he had developed a cloak-and-dagger mentality, so much so that one person described him to me as an amusing caricature.

He has been known by many names, most of which, according to John, begin with W: Wells, Watts, etc., but *Max* has been standard since 1967. He took the name inexplicably from *les max*, the name for French GIs during the Algerian war. Whatever his style or current alias, it is indisputable that Max has been highly effective in helping deserters and resisters, who need all the support they can get when the full weight of the military machine comes down on them.

When in 1967 the problem first presented itself, Max offered to take over the PACS *permanence* and in particular to handle the men. He worked hard to have the *bona fides* placed in homes and jobs throughout France; he had a good "network" of contacts and was effective in this. In February 1968 he staged an open conference for deserters.

For a while things went well. Other groups took an interest in the problem. A Catholic *abbé* offered one hundred jobs (since all were menial jobs and outside of Paris, there were no takers). The War Resisters League in London was helpful. For a time the issue became chic: "Everybody wanted his or her deserter," Maria said. "All sorts of people got involved, and many who knew the clandestine procedures of the Nazi resistance. There was a great cloak-and-dagger atmosphere—meetings at midnight and such." She laughed. "I don't know what the French were risking. Nothing, in fact."

The support from the left was forthcoming, even though, as Max said in a memo, intellectuals did not understand "these poorly educated kids of peasant stock without the vocabulary of leftist protest." The left could understand them, he wrote, no more than the American officers who were constantly looking for a "Red-organized agitator" behind them.

In the beginning the French Communists wanted to help. In 1967 they managed to raise perhaps $1000 to $2000 for deserters—a tidy sum in France. "But the interesting element of this," Max wrote, "is that none of the deserters wanted to be beholden to the Communist Party. When the deserters found out the money came from the Communists, they sent it back. . . . Deserters didn't know anything about the Communist movement, nor did they give a damn." In 1968 the Party ceased its efforts to be helpful. Not long ago when Maria had encountered a Party member at a gathering for the NLF she had asked, "Do you have word of our deserter friends?" He replied, "I was going to ask you the same thing."

But after the "events of 1968"—the student–worker rebellion of May and June—there was a serious setback. A new government policy emerged that would subject any foreigner engaging in political activity of which the Government disapproved to immediate and even uninvestigated deportation. The policy was in the hands of the Direction de Surveillance de Territoire (D.S.T.), an organization parallel to the CIA, with the difference that the D.S.T. has a domestic goon squad. Not only *actual* political activity, but simply *the appearance of such*, would subject foreigners to deportation.

Maria related a spectacular example of this.

When the Sorbonne was taken over in May 1968, the students made a room available to American deserters. Vietnam had, of course, been a major factor in triggering the rebellion, and providing the room seemed a good way to dramatize the issue. Deserters took it over gleefully and held a "twenty-four-hour *permanence*" there. And then they gave a press conference.

In attendance was Scofield Coryell, a freelance American journalist and sometime-contributor to the *Guardian* and other leftist publications. Coryell had been in a neighboring room covering other "events" and had simply wandered into the deserter event. Several months later on August 15, a Friday and the beginning of a long weekend when Paris had been evacuated, as it always is in August, Maria got a call from Coryell's wife. Coryell had been arrested, she said, summoned to the Prefecture for questioning concerning "supplementary information concerning his papers." He was kept overnight. On Saturday evening, Coryell appeared at his home with a gendarme at either side, informed his wife that he had been expelled from the country, and together they packed a bag. The following morning at 6 A.M. he was put on a plane at Orly for the United States.

For a year Coryell and his wife were separated, but in that time she prepared a dossier, tirelessly gathering statements from people who had known her husband and testified that he had never worked with American deserters. Coryell at last was able to rejoin his wife in London. With the dossier finally in order, they filed suit in a French court and won. In 1971 they returned to France. The authorities never stated a reason for Coryell's expulsion, but intimated only that it was because of his involvement with deserters. Even if this had been true, what a paradox it is for a country to provide political refuge to deserters, but hostile refuge (if there is such a thing) and simultaneously to harass those who appeared to help the deserter community!

Sweden, Maria maintained, had done better. The Swedes had learned that, to provide political asylum, you had to do more than simply let someone in. The government had taken steps to permit a degree of integration: free Swedish lessons, free education and housing. Even with these benefits, there were stirrings of discontent among the some 600 resisters in Sweden. The situation there has been toughest for penniless deserters.

The Coryell affair was the first sign of the crackdown in France which signaled a period of harassment that lasted until the summer of 1971. The end of the vindictiveness came, Maria said, with Nixon's imposition of the 10 percent surcharge. The United States had lost control. "France," she concluded, "became a bourgeois government."

In November 1968, PACS was banned. Some months later, prior to Nixon's visit to France, several deserters, one of whom was completely unpolitical, were picked up and sent to an Atlantic island for the duration of the Presidential visit. When they returned, they were told that they should be happy for the paid vacation and that if they made a legal squabble about it they would be deported.

In January 1969, Max was ordered to appear at the Prefecture. He was handed a deportation order, but he was able to appeal. (The details of the story that follows were later provided me by Max, though Maria related the essentials.)

On March 5, 1969, after Nixon had left France, Max went to the police station to inquire about his appeal. He was told that the police had been looking for him and that the order to deport him must go into effect immediately. It appeared to be a case of bureaucratic lag, and he managed to receive another stay. However, the police presented him with a statement to the effect that he acknowledged that he had been enjoined to cease all political activity. He refused to sign, demanding a clarification. "Am I not allowed to shout 'Vive la France'?" he asked. The police had no answer for him.

After some delay the clarification came: Max was called back and presented with the same statement—with an added Kafkaesque sentence to the effect that he did not know the exact nature of the political crime with which he had been charged. This time he signed. His lawyer wrote to seven French Presidential candidates, asking whether or not they felt Max should be deported. All, including Pompidou, replied that they abhorred the situation.

Max was buying a *Herald Tribune* on June 19, on the

Boulevard St. Germain when he was approached by four men, whom he described as looking like movie gangsters— muscular, young, one looking like a "fake hippie." They shouted at him, " Hé, Marcel. You're wanted for armed robbery!" and grabbed him. He yelled out, "This is a kidnapping! This is a kidnapping!" A gendarme approached, but then withdrew when he realized that the men were plainclothesmen. Max continued to yell, directing his shouts at the people in a nearby café.

He was taken to the Ministry of Interior, interrogated, and then thrown in prison. There he went on a hunger and thirst strike. But one day, unaccountably, he was told he was going to be freed. His wife, mother, and lawyers arrived at the prison for his release, only to find that for some strange reason the order was rescinded, and Max was to be deported to Austria *tout de suite*. The police called the Austrian Embassy to clear the extradition. Even though the embassy refused, since Max did not carry an Austrian passport, the police put Max in a car, took him to Orly Airport, and attempted to put him on an Austrian plane for Vienna. Max's lawyers ran out on the runway, arguing with the French police, thus distracting them, while Max yelled out to the pilot that his boarding was illegal, that he had no Austrian papers, and that the Austrian Embassy had disapproved the extradition. The pilot refused to board him, and he was returned to prison, to solitary.

The next day he was informed that he would be flown to Corsica (still part of metropolitan France) and there placed under house arrest. He felt that so long as he was not turned over to the Americans, he was master of the situation. The move took place, and he lived in a hotel outside Ajaccio under loose house arrest for a few months. He was then allowed to return to Paris. But on October 15, 1969, he was again snatched by eight plainclothesmen and this time successfully deported to Austria. In France, François Mitterand, the leader of the opposition, who had received 45 percent of the vote in a Presidential contest with deGaulle, asked the Minister of the Interior, Ramon Marcellin, about the deportation. Marcellin did not reply for eleven months.

In February 1970, Max returned illegally to Paris to take his doctoral exams. He was picked up again and deported to Austria. His case became a university scandal. In a predictable university scenario, he was defended by his friends with the majority of the faculty refusing to take a stand and the dean shilly-shallying.

Max went on to Heidelberg, where on March 7 he happened to hear on the radio that he would be permitted to return to Paris to take his exam. He received a weekend visa for this purpose. He arrived in Paris and passed his exam, refusing to shake hands with two examiners who had not supported him in the academic debate over his expulsion. He returned to Heidelberg, tailed by a Simca station wagon and a Renault—a discreet tail, Max called it, so discreet that the police knocked a girl off a scooter in an effort to keep up with him, and had to stop to telephone for instructions.

In September 1970, Ramon Marcellin finally replied in the National Assembly to Mitterand's question, calling Max a notorious rabble-rouser, and foreigner, part Lenin and part James Bond, an organizer of Maoist students, who even wore a Mao jacket to his doctoral exam. (Max wrote he was sure that he would have the reputation of a revisionist.)

And finally, on July 13, 1971, the Court quashed his expulsion. This resulted from a letter his wife had written to someone high up in the legal system of France. They were successful, Max said, because he was a *"monsieur"* with contacts, rather than a "poor flunky." On a typical day in Orly, he pointed out, seventeen persons are processed for deportation.

If the situation with the authorities was difficult, Maria felt the deserters themselves complicated it. They had gained a reputation in the past few years for irregularity, for refusal to do hard work, for not being easily employable. As a group they had little education: they were double dropouts, from school and from the Army. She saw them as young people who were carried along on a string of failures and asserted that early failures were absolutely devastating. She quoted Adler: "The neurotic man is the discouraged man."

This was why they were so "childish," why they had so little preparation for meeting the political problem of dropping out. Of course there were exceptions. She told us an amusing story about Jim Morrissey, the deserter with whom John had lived before he moved in with Annette. Morrissey had asked for an American passport and was refused. He then found out that the Irish would provide a passport to anyone who had one Irish grandparent. Jim had two. He got his passport and traveled all over Europe. When he returned to Paris, there was a note from the Prefecture asking him to come in. He did. He knew them well at the Prefecture. At the station he was informed that the American Embassy had sent notice that Morrissey was to be picked up for traveling around Europe without a passport. Morrissey pulled out his Irish passport, and they all had a big laugh. But Maria would write of John Herndon later: "Poor little fellow, he really is the totally alienated species of *kleiner Mann* that Alfred Doeblin wrote about."

Her analysis of deserters was as devastating as her analysis of France. She felt they had no moral sense as a group: "And where are they going to get it? They say to the Church: 'What do you know about our experience?' and they are right. But many of them are too far gone now."

But "We have never blamed the deserter," she said.

Mike was getting quite uncomfortable, and I was simply confused. How could this woman who had been so helpful to deserters appear to be so contemptuous of them? Her thoughts seem to manifest Max's opinion that the mannered left in France simply could not relate to the unsophisticated "flunkies"—or had she too simply been worn out by them?

John Herndon was to give me some insight on this later. "Maria was a help," he said. "If I came to Maria with a problem, she'd jump on it right away. If she didn't know, she'd call up a lawyer who did. Her attitude changes like the weather. One minute she's for you, and she'll help you. Next minute she's not. Then she is again ... and she ain't. But she's eighty years old now, and you have to take that into consideration too."

Before we left, I asked her, with all her troubles with deserters, was she for amnesty?

"Oh, absolutely," she said. "There is no chance to save any of them over here. They can lead no decent social existence in France, and there is no way to reclaim them as human beings other than repatriation."

I parted with Mike after he was unable to reach any of the people that a French contact had suggested for the airport encounter and returned to the Majestic Hotel. The ride on the *métro* was a pensive one. I was enthralled by the strength and Old World charm of Maria Jolas, but some of what she had said troubled me considerably. The idea of deserters as social cases as well as political cases was new to me, providing an expansion of the amnesty argument. Why should the dropouts be among the few who bore the legal burden of the war? Had not American society done enough to them? Was Lieutenant Calley to be lumped together with the exiles as the only Americans to be legally punished for this war? And was it not a curious twist that the opponents of amnesty argued that there were criminals and dope addicts among the deserters, without acknowledging that exile was driving many to it? Repatriation is the only way to reclaim the social cases as human beings, Maria had said. But I was more preoccupied with the stories of Max and Scofield Coryell. They were stories of police power used arbitrarily. Was that power going to be used against us? I wondered.

At the Majestic Hotel, Dave Mason of the Associated Press was just cleaning up his work and was about to leave. I asked him if anything had happened at the Peace Talks, and he replied, "Not much. More prisoner-of-war stuff." He handed me Porter's additional remarks. They began,

We had hoped you would use the interval since the last session for serious reflection and a reassessment of your *totally unrealistic position* here. Unfortunately, we have heard nothing from you today to indicate such an effort on your part. We see no sign yet that you are interested in anything except having your ultimatums accepted *in toto*. On the general substance of matters before us, you neither answer questions about your demands, nor seek information about our proposals.

Nor do we detect any constructive comment from you with regard to the rights of prisoners of war.

I did not read further.

It was a pleasant warm evening in Paris, and I decided to walk back with Dave to his office on the Rue du Berri. I was thinking about whether or not it was time to start leaking the story of John's departure, and at the AP office I called the hotel and put the question to Mike. We agreed that, if I could establish an understanding with whomever I talked that the story would not be spread around before Monday, I should go ahead. I decided the most sympathetic journalist would be Jon Randal of *The Washington Post*, whose office was on the floor below. I went down to see him and sounded him out about secrecy. He said he had worked places like the Middle East where underground stories were commonplace: "I may not have written many good stories in my life, but I've never betrayed a confidence." And so I told him about John Herndon. He asked me immediately who our French lawyer was. I said we had none. He suggested a close friend of his, Christian Bourget, who had been involved in the defense of Middle Eastern skyjackers and other political cases, and would be good for this. It was a stroke of luck, for I'd been uncertain about how the French side of the case could best be handled. Jon called him up, and I went right over to see him in Raspail.

Bourget offered to make an inquiry at the Ministry of Interior about the French attitude toward a deserter leaving France without a passport or American military documentation. I asked him please not to indicate a time or mode of departure. He shrugged his shoulders in a charming French way. "*Non, non. Theoriqué,*" he said.

It is thought that the origin of the proverb "Misery loves company" comes from a more wordy saying of Thomas à Kempis: "It is a consolation to the wretched to have companions in misery." John Herndon's companion in his tough second exile in France was Annette. On the face of it, it seemed odd that they would have stuck together for a year and a half, for it was a relationship that on her part was based on fear. For John, she was a source of support and a release for frustration, and love flowed genuinely from it, even though it did not sound like love when he talked to her.

John had told me in the Algerian restaurant on Wednesday that Annette had had a "rough life." She is the offspring of a cross-cultural, cross-religious marriage. Her French father is a retired colonel in the French Army who was raised in a strict Catholic household. Her American mother had grown up in a Protestant family in Philadelphia. They had met in Morocco where her father was stationed and her mother was a nurse, and were married under French law which stipulated that the wife must become a French national. The details of this early period are not known even to Annette. She knew only that the marriage never worked.

Her mother nevertheless wanted a child. When she became pregnant she decided to leave North Africa after the child was born. "She left right after she had me," Annette said. "She told my father she wanted to go home and see her family and that he could rejoin her in the States. He did, at my grandparents' house, but he was not welcomed. They took him in, but they did not want him. He tried to find work in Philadelphia. He's an engineer, and he has excellent diplomas. But no one recognized his diplomas. So he finally got up and went to New York, got a job with a man who had a French secretary. She said these diplomas are worth something. He did drafting, well, not even as good as drafting. Finally, he figured out a problem they had, figured it out immediately, so they gave him a good job engineering, and he moved back to Philly.

"I don't know exactly why, but Mother left him. She asked him for child support, but he didn't give it. Never gave us a cent. The police were coming to get my father. He found out about it at the place where he worked, and he left on a plane for France, just before the police were coming to get him.

"He got a job in Paris and, again for a reason I don't know, my mother joined him there. They moved out into the suburbs. She stayed six months, said she wanted to visit her family in the States, left, and never came back. They were formally divorced under French law. Now he owns a little phosphate company here. Father came from a peasant family, and he's close to the soil. He loves plants and things. He's the highest person in this little town. He has a lot of influence and a lot of money. My mother died when I was fifteen."

In the meantime Annette grew up in Germantown in Philadelphia. She went to Germantown High School, which was half black and half white at that time, and there she befriended a black boy who had substantial white blood in him. Annette had felt sorry for him because the other blacks taunted him and the whites did not associate with him. He was a little sick, she said. One day when she was sixteen, she was walking home from school with him, and he led her across a vacant lot—right into a trap. She was gang-raped by eight blacks. "It was his way of getting back at the white race," Annette said. She became pregnant.

In the hospital Annette was hypertense. The pregnancy could have resulted from several episodes. When she caught a glimpse of the black baby, she had a nervous breakdown. To calm her down the staff kept her on tranquilizers to which she became addicted and eventually she had to cold turkey. Without support, with her mother dead, and with a child to care for now, Annette needed help. In an old address book of her mother's, she found her father's address in France. She wrote to him, and he asked her to come to France. This she did and had been there for six years. For a time it worked out all right. Annette lived with him and got a maid's job in a school in Paris. But then there was a falling out. She got an apartment in the city, for herself and her child, Carol, but her father refused to give the child up. The separation became legalized, and Annette was permitted to visit Carol only once a month.

"You see, I look exactly like my mother, and he hated my mother. At first, when he saw me in the States, he loved me, but now he feels that, since I left him, I'm doing the same thing to him my mother did. He sees me as the same person as my mother, and he pretty well hates me.

"But he had left us for fifteen years, didn't come to see us, didn't send us any money. That's pretty bad. So raising my kid is the only way in the eyes of the French that he can redeem himself."

One of the strangest elements of this unspeakable situation is that Annette describes her father as a "very, very prejudiced man," who "agrees absolutely with what the Germans did to the Jews in the Second World War." She tells of an incident when she was scheduled to see Carol. She had bought a little black doll and baked some small cakes to give her, but when she arrived at her father's house, there was no one home. They had left deliberately. It was snowing. Annette waited as long as she could, and then she left the package for the child on the steps. Four weeks later, the same package came back to her in the mail; the cakes were rotten; the clothes on the doll were ripped off and there was a note enclosed in the scrawl of the woman Annette's father lived with: "I know you're partial to the blacks, but one nigger in the family is enough." Annette fainted.

She took the case into the French court, filing suit against her father for the custody of her child. The lines were drawn: half-foreign maid living with American deserter vs. established engineer and colonel in the reserves. That is where the situation stood in that week in March.

"When I first came to live with her," John told me, "she never used the word 'love.' She didn't like or love very many people in her life. She didn't feel comfortable using the word. After we'd been together for about three months, we went out to dinner, came back, and she told me she loved me. She said it like she really meant it. . . like for the first time in her life, she really knew what the meaning of the word was. . . . She'd never loved anybody before, I know that. I bought her a present at Christmas, and she sat there and cried and cried, just like a kid. Beautiful. She'd never had a Christmas present before. She really felt sorry because she didn't get me a present, but you know how it is. . . .

"She had lived with somebody else before, for a couple a

months. But she couldn't joke around with him. He was a real serious type. She was afraid of him. Actually, Annette is afraid of any man. She don't like to get hurt. She's real timid. She used to let other people do her thinking for her, until I came to live with her. Now she's a very smart woman. Nobody's gonna pull the wool over my baby's eyes."

While I was seeing Christian Bourget in Raspail, two plain-clothesmen arrived at Annette and John's apartment in the H.L.M. Annette was alone. They identified themselves as being from the Prefecture of the 13ᵉ Arrondissement. Annette let them in, for it states in her rental contract that the police have the right to make checks. It also states in the contract that no resident is permitted to do political work, that only members of the renting family were permitted to reside in the apartment, and that the resident is required to spend annually as much on furniture and repairs as he does on rent:

One of the two showed his badge, and the interrogation began:

"You're the one who asked custody for your daughter?"

"Yes."

"You do political work?"

"Who me? I don't do political work."

"There's this friend of yours who lives here. Friend's name is David?"

"No, his name is John."

"Give me all your papers. Your passports. Your pay slips." (Pay slips indicate how much a person receives monthly.)

"How many pay slips?"

"All of them."

"All of them?"

"Yes."

She went into the bedroom and came back with them. He looked at the top slip.

"What month is this for?"

"February '72."

"How much do you make? Around 900 francs?"

"Yes."

"Is John working?"

"He's helping a carpenter near Bastille."

"Where?"

"I don't know."

"How much does he make there?"

"Around 700 francs."

"Where is your friend's passport?"

"He doesn't have a passport."

"Doesn't have a passport!"

"No. If he did, I couldn't give it to you anyway. It's not mine."

"Is John a deserter?"

"I can't say he's a deserter. That's a legal question. He's AWOL."

"Do you know any other deserters?"

"AWOLs?"

"Yes."

"I know a few."

"What kind of work do your friends do?"

"I don't know exactly."

"I don't think you should associate with people who don't have steady jobs, if you want custody of the kid."

"Do you really think that could hurt the custody case?"

"Yeah, it would be bad for the case . . . . Does John have a right to stay here?"

"Here in France? Yes, he has a *carte de séjour*. You should be able to find that out at the Cité [central records in Paris]."

"Does John drink sometimes?" (Annette said to me later, "They could find that out at the local café—and how!")

"Yes."

"Do you drink?"

"No."

"Does he have a weapon?"

"No. I haven't even seen him with a pocket knife."

"Does he shoot up drugs?"

"No."

"Do you?"

"No. If you have any doubts, take all the tests immediately. I prefer you take them now, if you have any doubts."

The other cop laughed at that. He was snide.

"And you really think you want to take your daughter to live here," he said.

Annette did not answer.

"This place isn't very big." (To me, she said, "Just because an apartment is not good enough for a couple doesn't mean that they won't rent it to you. The apartment's rated as a family unit!") " . . . Place isn't big enough for the kid. Has no comforts. No hot water. Toilet in the hallway. How much rent do you pay?"

"Less than 100 francs a month."

"What are you going to do with your daughter while you work?"

"She'll go to school while I work. She can eat with me there. There's a stove, and I have a right to do cooking."

"There's not much furniture in here."

No answer from Annette.

"You painting here?" (He was trying to be friendly now.)

"Yes."

"You might start by painting the table."

They left. It was a simple case of harassment. The police had been to their apartment only once before—after John had written a letter to Mme. Nguyen Thi Binh, the NLF foreign minister, but that time they had posed as researchers, doing a work survey. John came in an hour later. Annette was too frightened to tell him. The following day she did not tell him either, too frightened at the thought of what he might do *because* she had not told him.

What had kept them together for a year and a half is beyond my ken. But probably, even in the deterioration of their relationship when Annette took to making fun of John when he would come home drunk, he still was fulfilling a basic need in her. He had in fact mentioned to her the possibility of giving himself up as early as May 1970, after he had been fired by Levy and had been unable to get another job for several months. But she had pleaded with him to wait until amnesty was declared. John said Annette would do anything to gain custody of her child. And they had discussed the possibility of snatching Carol and making a run for it.

★ FRIDAY, MARCH 17 ★

I met with Mike Uhl the first thing in the morning to check on scheduling. The pace was steadily quickening, and

Friday was packed with appointments. At 12:30 we were expected for lunch at the Quaker Center, where I would finally have a chance to talk with Tony Clay. At 2:15 John and I would leave for Rouen by train. It would be his farewell to the French friends in Rouen who had helped him when he first arrived. I was anxious to see how John got along with French people. It would be a way of judging his degree of integration into French life. We would stay overnight in Rouen and take the morning train back.

Mike informed me that CBS was ready to do the story, but Peter Kallisher, the chief CBS correspondent in Paris, had been assigned to it instead of Steve Young. It appeared to be a case of pulling rank. Kallisher would be at the hotel at 11 A.M. to discuss plans. He had expressed the desire to accompany us to Rouen, and Mike wanted to know my feelings. I said I had no objections to having cameras in Rouen, but that I needed to be alone with John on the two-hour trip. We still had much to discuss.

Kallisher arrived. He is a small man; perhaps 5'5", with graying sideburns and a husky, melodious voice. He was elegantly attired in a suit and ascot and commented on what a glorious day it was for a trip to Normandy. We set up plans for his cameraman to meet the train in Rouen and shoot our arrival. Then in the evening, Kallisher wanted to shoot John together with his friends. John, the star of the show, ambled in at noon, dressed in his sweater-dungaree-jackboot uniform. We introduced him to Kallisher, and then Mike, John, and I caught a cab for the Quaker Center.

Tony Clay fulfilled my every expectation of what a selfless, dedicated pacifist might be. Lean and tall, with gray hair, a gray, well-kept beard, and water-blue eyes, he has a saintly El Greco face. He describes himself as a retired carpenter from Sussex of working-class background, and the biblical reference is inescapable. Maria Jolas had told me that he was a man who had simply been worn out by the deserters in the endless, thankless job of fathering these "children," corresponding with them in prison, dealing with the authorities when they were in trouble, giving them a few francs lest they starve. John described him as the most impressive figure he had ever met. "Tony used to say," John said, "we don't write rules down. You live them first and then you write them down."

We had a quick lunch, and then Tony and I withdrew to his quarters for the twenty minutes that we had to talk. He began by telling me about the three organizations that were involved in supporting deserters. (Tony Clay was not a particularly good person to analyze this organizational situation, and Safe Return refused to go into the matter in detail for obvious reasons.) The American Deserters Committee (ADC) encouraged soldiers to desert and was active in countries which offered asylum. In Sweden the Committee had split into Maoist and Trotskyite factions. War Resisters International had a five-point program: write the President, legislators, and military commanders about the war; stage walkouts from bases; participate in public demonstrations against the war; desert; apply for conscientious objector status. Finally, Rita Act (Resistance in the Army: Act!), Max's "baby," embraced all of the above as legitimate forms of protest, and added the printing of anti-war GI newspapers, and by implication, "fragging," the physical violence against hated officers and non-coms. "Do the thing you think is best" is Rita Act's motto.

Then we had a rather sobering talk about John. According to Tony, he would never integrate into the French society. He had made no effort to learn French. Without the language, integration was utterly impossible. John had survived between jobs by bumming money or "touches," as Tony called them. (John later admitted that soft touches or hustling was an easier method of survival than working in France under the circumstances of exile.) Tony had simply tried to be loving and patient with him. What had been his ambition for John? "If he could get a steady job and could be a good husband, a miracle would have been achieved," he said.

Tony had the impression that in the States money had come easily to John and that he had disposed of it easily. But in France money is hard to come by, and "If you're in the habit of spending it easily, then you're in trouble." John had had a very tough period in the previous six months.

"He's in danger of becoming an alcoholic," Tony told me. "He's never been robust."

John too had talked to me about his slide: "I got to the point where I really didn't give a damn. I was living from day to day more or less. I never worried about the drinking. Annette worried about it. Every weekend I used to go down to the café and get ripped on Saturday and Sunday with my Vietnamese friends. I noticed I was getting more hostile toward Annette. It was pretty rough on her."

John's good side, Tony said, was his generosity. He'd tried to help others, had put them up, and tried to find work for them. In fact, it was John's generosity that had brought on the nadir of his fortunes in France.

In November 1971, a deserter called Lewis Plyler came to France. He had no place to go and no job, so John and Annette took him in at the H.L.M. He slept on the cement floor.

"Lewis knew that when I left the house, he left the house," John said. "When I came home, he came home. If he got home before me, he would usually wait outside. If Annette was there, he wouldn't go in."

Plyler grew tired of his situation rather quickly and made contact with a lawyer in England about returning home. This he did before Christmas 1971, and he was still in pre-trial confinement when we returned to the States, awaiting a general court-martial for desertion.

On New Year's Eve, a Friday, John went to a café near the H.L.M., and the owner demanded 200 francs. It was Plyler's debt, and he had told the owner that John would pay it. The owner threatened John, saying if he didn't get the money that he (the owner) "would take care of" John. John knew he had a gun on him. "I was very, very low," John said, "Under a lotta strain. With Lewis's debt, everything had come together at one time, but it had been building up for quite a few months."

John went to the school where Annette worked, and demanded 200 francs from her. He did not tell her why he needed it. She refused, and he pushed her down, shouting and threatening her. In tears, she gave him the money, but said she never wanted to see him again. John went immediately to the café and paid Plyler's debt, and then went home to the H.L.M. Annette did not come home. She was hiding out at a friend's house. "I didn't eat or sleep for three days," John said, "On Monday I went to where she worked and they wouldn't let me talk to her. I left a note telling her to meet me in a café. She didn't show up. I got drunk and uptight. So I cut my arm in front of the school. Then I went over and seen Tony. Tony took me to a doctor and got me a hotel room. He told me I looked like a wreck. Then he set up an appointment to meet Annette. So me and Annette got together. There wasn't that much said. Lotta crying going on, that's about it."

It was not a serious attempt to end his life, Tony said. John had cut himself on the forearm well above his wrist. But neither was it easily dismissed. He carries an ugly scar from the incident still. Annette wrote me later about the meeting between them that Tony had arranged.

"John looked so sad, and he promised to be good, so I gave in, and we started living together again. I tried to get him to go to the doctor for his drinking, but he wouldn't hear about it, so he started getting drunk as usual."

John has great difficulty in looking back at this incident. After the attempt on his life, he recalls painfully, "I was afraid of myself, of what I could do to myself. It was funny because everybody was afraid of me ... even me. Tony told me, 'You walk down the street, you look like you're going to kill somebody.' "

I asked Tony about John's relationship with Annette. Annette, he thought, was less interested in John than he was in her. John treated her as inferior, a kind of sergeant-major to private relationship. He'd used her, but she was deceptively strong, Tony said. "Threats and lies are part of John's armory of survival."

It was a harsh statement, but Tony, who had accepted thanklessly the burden of keeping John going during his long exile, was entitled to make it. Threat of starvation does not bring out the best in people. "The wretched seldom make cheerful company," Carlyle wrote. I asked Tony what his hope for John was.

"He must get back to his own environment, so that he can put the brakes on himself. Otherwise he'll just go downhill."

It was time to go. John and I caught a cab for St. Lazare. Along the way I asked him if it was true that Tony had been worn out by deserters. He replied that Tony had been particularly down in 1969 when there had been a lot of hard drug problems. He got very tired that year and told a group of deserters that he'd had enough of them. "But he's stable now," John said.

The train left St. Lazare and followed the Seine west through the suburbs of Paris and into the valleys of Normandy. During the two-hour trip to Rouen John and I settled down to talk about his political career in France. For clearly John was a political case now, even if he had been one of Maria's social cases as well. He was becoming a political case of national significance, and yet it was coming about almost by accident, without John's inviting it. Occasionally along the way, he broke our concentration to comment on the scenery—a good place for fishing here, a beautiful view there, "if only they would cut down the trees so we could see it."

"When we come into France, we're told that we can stay here as long as we keep quiet. We sign a statement when we arrive stating that we will not do any political work or be present at any *manifestations*" (demonstrations; any group must get permission from the French police to hold a demonstration.) "Any deserter who demonstrates openly can get in big trouble."

"The first trip to France I didn't do any political work. Max was never one to push. He said I could do political work if I wanted to, but I didn't get around to it until the second trip. Then I started making contacts"— "contacts" is a word that crept into John's conversation constantly; he marveled at Max's contacts—"and started to take care of people. That takes a lot of time. This man comes in, and he knows no French whatsoever. You have to take him around, get him a *carte de séjour*. Mostly what it consists of is waiting in line."

John's political work consisted chiefly of briefing other deserters when they arrived in the country, helping them legalize their status if they wanted to stay, or trying to set things up if they wanted to move on to Canada or Sweden. He told one story of a deserter who wanted to go to Canada, but whom Rita Act could not manage to buy the plane ticket, "so we sent him back to his unit in Germany. The same damn night the Gay Liberation movement came to my house at 3 o'clock in the morning, soaking wet from the rain, saying, 'Look, we got a plane ticket to send him to Canada. . . .' Very nice people. I could ask them to keep someone if I wanted. I know I can always jam someone there in an emergency. I'm not going to look down on someone that's doing his thing. But it does make you feel kind of funny. . . . A free ticket to Canada from the Gay Liberation Movement."

John also received mail for Rita Act. In the spring of 1971, he gave an interview to the Rita Act newspaper on POW conditions at the camp outside Bien Hoa where he'd been a guard. On the back page of the same issue of the paper was emblazoned:

ANTI-WAR LITERATURE IS A SAFE CONDUCT PASS. CARRY THIS WITH YOU AT ALL TIMES IN NAM. THE COMMANDER OF THE SOUTH VIETNAMESE PEOPLE'S LIBERATION ARMED FORCES HAS ORDERED: THAT GI'S WHO BY THEIR VISIBLE ACTIONS SHOW THEY ARE AGAINST THE WAR ARE NOT TO BE ATTACKED, THAT GI'S WHO CARRY ANTI-WAR LITERATURE BE TREATED AS FRIENDS NOT ENEMIES, THAT GI'S WHO ACTIVELY SUPPORT THE STRUGGLE OF THE VIETNAMESE PEOPLE BE AIDED AS BROTHERS. CARRY THIS WITH YOU, IT MAY SAVE YOUR LIFE.

The basis for this information was a press conference given by Mme. Nguyen Thi Binh, the foreign minister of the National Liberation Front and their Negotiator at Paris, on April 31, 1971. She declared that "the South Vietnamese people and its armed forces are disposed to cease fire on American soldiers who do not undertake hostile actions against them," and invited American soldiers to negotiate local cease-fires with opposing forces. Later, Mme. Binh's

Tôi căm thù chiến tranh xâm lược này. Tôi không chịu chiến đấu nhân dân Việt Nam.

I AM AGAINST THE WAR AND WILL NOT FIGHT THE VIETNAMESE PEOPLE

SAVE YOUR LIFE

This literature, if found on a GI, will save his life with NFL forces.

spokesman Duong Dinh Thao, said that such truces had been commonplace among opposing Vietnamese in many areas throughout the war. The purpose of the order, put out to all NLF troops earlier in the week, he said, was to "create conditions for U.S. soldiers and officers to escape the war."

April 31 was a big day for Vietnam. President Nixon said of the tens of thousands of anti-war demonstrators who had disrupted Washington for ten days, "The Congress is not intimidated. The President is not intimidated." (It was in the vein of his 1969 Moratorium statement, when 500,000 Americans demonstrated on the Mall: "Under no circumstances will I be influenced by them.") On April 31 Captain Eugene M. Kotouc was acquitted of maiming a VC suspect outside My Lai. The court-martial board believed him when he claimed that he had cut off the finger of a suspect "accidentally" during an interrogation while threatening him with a hunting knife. This left only Captain Ernest Medina to be acquitted. On the same day Representative Ronald Dellums ended four days of hearings on U.S. war crimes, an event which was largely organized by Mike Uhl and Tod Ensign. They had heard scores of GIs testifying to war crimes that they had witnessed or committed, and an Army spokesman said that the criminal investigating units would "look into the allegations." While this was going on in the States, at the Paris Peace Confrence, Negotiator David Bruce, in a statement nearly identical to William Porter's a year later, said, "In the case of our side, the International Red Cross regularly visits your men at places of their detention. But there has been no inspection of conditions of internment of prisoners of war held by your side." He urged a third country or international body to do so. And back in Washington, Representative William Anderson of Tennessee, who had investigated the tiger-cage situation earlier in the year, disclosed that day that $400,000 more in U.S. tax money was being used to build more tiger cages.

Mme. Binh's press conference was perhaps lost in all that news for the American public, but it was to make John Herndon something of a celebrity within the anti-war movement in Europe, and even somewhat in the United States. For he wrote Mme. Binh a letter the following day:

May 1, 1971
Paris, France

Mme Nguyen Thi Binh
Commandant-adjoint des FAPL
c/o Gouvernement revolutionnaire provisoire
39, Avenue Georges Mandel
Paris XVI

Dear Madame Nguyen Thi Binh:
We are a group of Americans who are on unauthorized leave here in the Paris area. I myself served in Vietnam from 1966–68. I thought we were there to keep the peace. When I was on R&R (rest and recreation) in Phug Tau, I talked to a lot of Vietnamese. We always thought they were with the NLF. You really had to hand it to them. They explained that if all the foreign troops would leave Vietnam, the Vietnamese people would make peace themselves and decide on the kind of government they wanted. This is the first time that the U.S. Army has had a Revo-

lutionary Army in front of them and they don't know how to cope with them. A lot of the GIs think more of the NLF than they do of their own commanding officers. If I was asked to go to Vietnam now, I would be glad to do so if there was some way it could help the Vietnamese people. I understand very well that there are GIs now fighting with the NLF.

While some of us resist inside the Army, some of us have gone on prolonged leave until the Vietnam War is over. We are in a weird new unit here in Paris. We really appreciated Duong Dinh Thao's press conference. He picked up all the points we are working on; we send out anti-war literature; we put out a newsletter called ACT here in Paris and we like to think some GI's life may be saved because he is carrying some ACTs around with him. We also help soldiers who desert, whether for political reasons, or because of a lot of harassment in the Army because of racism or some guy pulling rank, or both. We think this open declaration of your support for our struggle, inside and outside the Army, is great. We really feel we're fighting together with the Vietnamese people to end this war now.

We hope you won't mind that we are sending this as an open letter. We think a lot of GIs, in and out of the Army, feel like we do, and that we are talking for a lot of others besides ourselves. If there is any way in which our support here in Paris can be of help to you, please call on us.

> E-5, Sgt. John Herndon (temporarily self-retir'd)
> RA 13996407
> Vietnam veteran

The letter appeared shortly after in *L'Humanité,* the French Communist paper, as well as in the Rita Act paper, *The Great Speckled Bird,* in Atlanta; the *South Vietnam Courier,* released by the NLF; and *BOND,* the American Servicemen's Union newspaper.

Why had he written the letter?

"I felt that personally I had to thank her for her press conference. She said that the NLF would honor any type of anti-war literature as a pass for any American GI who deserted in Vietnam. It would be safe conduct, and he would be treated accordingly. So I felt I had to write her a letter and thank her, 'cause you don't know how many lives might be saved by that."

This was not the first time that John had been involved with the Communists, but it was limited involvement of dubious value to John or the Communists. His statements indicated what Maria had said: that he didn't give a damn about the theory or persuasion of Communism, but looked upon the party as one resource for survival among many. He said his involvement dated back to 1969. He would go around to various Communist printers occasionally in the period that followed and ask them to print one thing or another.

"All of them," he said, "were willing to help me as far as printing stuff. But they want you to do work that is completely open, completely out front, and I can't do this, because I'd get expelled from France."

His analysis of the movement went as follows: "There's your Lenin-believers, your Stalin-believers, your Mao Tse Tung–believers. . . . But the French Communist is the most dedicated Communist in the world. I've talked with Communists from other countries, but the French are the most dedicated. If they had made 100 francs a month, they'd give 70 francs to the Communist Party."

Had they ever asked him to join?

"No. They haven't. Never been approached. And I've been helped by all persuasions, fascists included. Even they have hearts too to a certain extent, so it's hard for me to say this or that group is the best. Maybe some other deserter can say these people are bad, these people are good, but I can't say that, because I've been helped by both. . . . So it comes down to the way the person felt, if they're sympathetic toward somebody who's starving. . . . Even the fascists are concerned for the people who're getting squashed. So you let the fascist know that you think you're going to get squashed, and let him take you under his wing."

As political parties of different persuasions had drifted in and out of John's experience as an exile, so had prominent people. "They're just the lucky ones," John said, "They've succeeded in life so far, but they put their pants on the same way you do."

On Mme. Binh: "I went over to see her with Mary Richardson of the Black Caucus. Mary and Mme. Binh did most of the talking. Mme. Binh was very, very friendly. She's a very, very smart woman. They discussed black people in general: How they were discriminated against in America. Mme. Binh agreed. Black people were just like Vietnamese people. Anyhow, that's the conclusion they come to and everyone was happy. Desertion never came into it. Everybody got an NLF pin and a ring, and that was about the extent of the conversation."

On Mary McCarthy: "She's a very beautiful person. She's a good contact. Anything I want to do—if she likes the idea, she'll support part of it."

On Mark Lane: "I was supposed to be in his book [*Conversations with Americans*]. But I couldn't recognize myself. I can see why the critics tore him apart. He talked about a jump school in Memphis, Tennessee, and there ain't none there. I wrote his publisher a letter."

On Melina Mercouri: "She's a big actress, but it's not like she's something special. She's a person like everybody else. She wanted to know how I'd left the Army and why I'd left the Army. She said it was a beautiful thing I done. She's a beautiful person."

On Jane Fonda: "I went to a press conference of hers. These guys were there that had silk, mohair suits on, saying 'Jane, can I have 5 minutes,' and I walked up to her in what I have on now, and said, 'Jane, can I talk to you?' and she got up and walked out and we talked for forty-five minutes about what Rita was doing in France. I was dressed just like this. The only difference was, instead of a pack of cigars in my boot, I had an *International Herald Tribune*, and I had an old paratrooper's jacket on that had holes in it that I made all my jumps in. And everybody looked at me, and said, 'Who the hell is he?' 'Who's he that he can go up and say, "Hey Jane, can I talk to you awhile?"' and here I sit with a pocket full of 500-franc notes and a beautiful suit, and I can't even see her for five minutes?' She was beautiful, she really was. It's the idea that she don't consider herself too good.... Good is not the word. They have the word 'bourgeois' over here."

On Joan Baez: "She's a little different. She impressed me a little bit. She doesn't make the harsh statements like Jane Fonda. She sung at this Festival of Humanity the Communist Party has here, but she seemed like she was kind of tense. Perhaps her thoughts were someplace else."

But the celebrities were not always helpful. "Oh, there's always people around who try to manipulate you a little bit. If we wanted something political to happen, you couldn't get ahold of these people. And then when it started to happen, all of a sudden, there they'd be, trying to manipulate it, and always trying to get credit for creating it."

And the students with whom he came into almost daily contact were not always comprehensible. "They use these $50- and $35-words. Lot of 'em I still can't understand. But I picked up quite a few of 'em just being around. But when I first came to France, I was lost. I didn't know what they were talking about."

Nonetheless, "Paris," John said, "is my release."

"I can say what I want to say in Paris. I can talk to anybody I want to talk to. I can say anything I wanta say. If it offended somebody, the hell with him. I could sit down and argue with a guy for six hours, and we could get up and be friends. As far as I'm concerned I am really free over here. American government can't touch me. The French government don't bother me. This is the place to start a movement, believe me."

How then did he approach his return home?

"I feel I have something to do. I have something to say. I just need people to say it to. And the United States is the place to start—at the root of the problem. If I did nothing more than to open up the minds of some of the people in America, I'd think I'd succeeded."

With the TV cameras about to roll and talk of a nationwide special on him, John had developed a fanciful notion of becoming an issue in the Presidential primaries. I tried to divest him of this idea and we talked further about amnesty.

"Of course, what I hope will result from this is a general amnesty. 'Course, you never know, but at least the American people would learn that there's quite a few thousand of us still in exile, wanting to come home, if they'll only do something about it. It's up to them to pick the person who will let us come home. In some sort of way if I can only get the backing of the American people in order to declare an amnesty to allow draft resisters and deserters to come back to the United States and live a normal life without any prosecution whatever, with . . . no alternative service."

I explained to John the distinction between general and universal amnesty, for he was under the same misapprehension as most Americans that "general amnesty" meant blanket, unconditional amnesty. It does not. Universal amnesty is the proper historical term for amnesty without prosecution, without alternative service, without any conditions whatever. General amnesty means conditions, like Senator McGovern's proposal for a case-by-case analysis of deserters. The distinction, I told John, came from the Civil War. Presidents Lincoln and Johnson had each declared general amnesty proclamations, granting conditional pardon to those involved in the Confederate cause. But the relevant historical precedent to the Vietnam situation was Andrew Johnson's Universal Amnesty Proclamation of December 24, 1868. It was a one-sentence declaration—all that would be needed in our own time—which declared unconditionally a full pardon to anyone who directly or indirectly participated in the "late insurrection." Universal amnesty, rather than general amnesty, was what John was talking about, and I was anxious for him to use the proper term when he went before the TV cameras.

I cautioned John that the American people might pay attention to his case and they might not; but even if they did, their attention span would be short. Amnesty, I said, is a very emotional issue in the United States now, and I told him about my appearance on the Owen Spann talk show in San Francisco, answering questions for two hours about my advocacy of universal amnesty. At first, I explained, the questions were gentle and sympathetic, but as time progressed, they grew tougher and more bitter, laced with the words "cowardice" and "treason."

"This is what we're trying to change, correct," John said. "You got to force the issue and this is the perfect time. We're forcing it, and let's hope it comes to the best. If it don't, we haven't lost anything, right? Even if I have to spend time in a stockade. it won't be a total loss. Even in the stockade I'm still associating with people. I can still speak. Even if they put me in the box, somebody still goin' to come peepin' in at me. I can say what I want to say, when I want to say it. Maybe a year, maybe I pull a year. It still hasn't stopped me in that year from getting my word across. Anyway, if I'm wakin' up 500 people, I've done it as far as I'm concerned."

Would any deserters go back on a conditional amnesty? John thought a few would, but the conditions proposed so far applied only to draft resisters:

"Taft and McGovern came out with something nice, but it's only for draft resisters. What they're saying is, so far as I'm concerned, if there was another world war and these guys refused to go into the service, that's O.K., they refused to go in. But the guys who went in, went to Vietnam and done their thing, and then refused to go back . . . fergit em. Fergit em! They committed the unforgivable sin."

I asked John what the exiles in France would do if there were no amnesty.

"They're going to continue to do what they've been doing. They're going to try to help people who're coming in. They're going to do their little bit."

"And what about you, what do you think will happen to you?"

"I figure they'll sock it to me with a discharge and get me out to cut down on the publicity, but then they'll just be opening the wall. They don't realize it, but they opened it up. That's what we want. That's the idea of the game." He was certainly right about that

"What will you do if you're discharged?"

"Well, I have to come back to France and pick up my fiancée. We have to fight the legal hassle with her father.

Once we get custody, well, we'll go back. I'd love to settle down close to my family in Baltimore. Baltimore is a central area. It sets about thirty-three miles from Washington, D.C., where the Pentagon is located. Inside of Maryland you have the Aberdeen Proving Ground, where they teach demolitions, you have Fort Holabird where they train the CIA, you have Fort Meade, which is a training center for pigs...MPs... and where one of the My Lai trials took place. So it's a good place to operate.

"I'd start at the root, the GI. I got a little bit of money at home. As far as I know there's no central meeting place for GIs in Baltimore. I'd like to start a place like that, a coffee house, if you want to call it that, but more like a restaurant. Cheap meals...conversation...stuff to read so you can make up your own mind."

"Cheap wine?"

"It'd be a problem with the wine. They got an age limit on wine, you see, and I don't want to cut myself away from the seventeen-, eighteen-, nineteen-year-olds."

"But what if the Vietnam war is over?" I asked. Would he still want to work with GIs?

"It's beyond Vietnam. The Army should be like a job, so the GI looks at the time he spent in the military as work, not as something he had to do, something he lost time in as far as life goes. Life is pretty short for some. There'd be no such a thing as passes and all this. From what everybody's told me, the Communist is the one that keeps track of the people, keeps them behind barbed wire and the wall. The military's doing the same thing. They have their little wall. You go out, you got to have a pass. There's gate guards— that's a wall. They're talkin' about stopping Communism, and as far as I'm concerned, they got it right there in America!"

"But what if there's a volunteer army?"

"Even if there's a voluntary service, the Army's still going to need a few changes. Something's going to go wrong. Somebody's going to try to get hard, tough. So setting up a coffee house's no loss. So if they're volunteers or not, they can get together and talk, discuss the subject they want to discuss, without somebody coming up and saying well, you can't talk about that."

We were approaching Rouen. A Frenchman in the opposite seat, a balding little man with a screwed-up face, tapped John on the shoulder, pointing to a large factory along the river. After some time, John understood: it was a chocolate factory. We had five minutes before coming into the station. I asked John if he was nervous about the TV cameras.

"I've been on TV before," he said and told me of the time in October 1969 when he and Jim Morrissey had gone to England to do two fifteen-minute programs on desertion and exile for the BBC. Their *cartes de séjour* had been sufficient documentation for the trip. "Look at it this way. These people are just ilke you. And if they're working for you, it should be even less of a problem. There's no point about being nervous about it. If you have something to say ... you know what you're doing is right ... the hell with whoever don't like it."

We arrived on time at 3:30 in Rouen, a city of 400,000 built on the banks of the meandering Seine, and a place of ominous historical reference for John, for it was the medieval bastion of the English-supported Burgundians where Joan of Arc was burned at the stake. In one of her interrogations, she was asked,

"Does God hate the English?"

"I know nothing of the hatred or the love of God for the Englishmen," she had replied, "but this I know: that they will soon be all thrust out of France, save those of them who leave their bodies here."

The TV cameras were ready on the platform as we disembarked. People on the train popped their heads out of the windows to stare at this unlikely celebrity. We went on to the town's famous cathedral where the crew filmed John and me, looking up at the spire on the tower many hundreds of feet above us, a tower built in the Middle Ages by selling indulgences to the people so they might eat butter during Lent.

We stood before it in the sunlight, with the cameras

rolling, talking about how John's friends had brought him there after they had taken him in. Kallisher would arrive later and be irritated that I had been included in the picture. After the shooting was over, we left the camera crew and walked inside. A pathetic, wizened woman approached us, with her hand outstretched. John reached in his pocket and handed her a franc. I knew he only had ten francs to his name.

"She's probably a wino," he said, "but even winos have to eat."

We wandered about, John consumed with a great sense of wonder about the stained glass and the chapels. About an elaborate wooden confession booth, John said, "Imagine how many hours it must've taken him. He really knew what he was doing. If that ain't a museum piece ..."

Later when we walked down the cobblestone Rue de la Gross Horloge under the clock that had been mounted in 1396, past the town belfry, John was buoyant, and I realized that coming to Rouen had relieved the pressure of Paris for both of us. We ran into the CBS cameraman, Joe Masraff, a very amusing Frenchman who speaks perfect American English. He bought us each an ice cream cone and related how he and Kallisher had been pursuing Ambassador Watson the day before for a comment on the Anderson drunkenness story. When they finally caught the diplomat, Watson had scowled and refused to comment,

"He was so stupid about it," Joe said, "He should have treated it as a gag, and said something like, 'If you had to deal with the Chinese, you'd have to get drunk once in a while too.'" It seemed a very French way of looking at it.

We lost Joe in the Vieux Marche where Joan of Arc was burned, and then we went on and got a hotel room.

At 5:30 we went off to catch a bus for the apartment of John's friends. We got lost at first and ended up on the wrong side of the Seine. When we found out our mistake, we crossed back over again. On the bridge we passed the pathetic, bentover woman of the cathedral, walking upright at a brisk pace and pulling a cart crammed with groceries behind her, and John chuckled at the sight. Later he said, "The suspense is building. I talk now with a tickle in my voice. But this is almost as good as being back in America."

He practiced his yodeling, West Virginia style, which he said he'd gotten down pretty well when he was picking grapes in the South. Then when we caught the bus which, packed with people, labored up a long and very steep hill above the city, he began to sing. "Well, I wish I was in Louisiana. Down by Texarkana . . ."

On the summit the bus made a long horseshoe turn around a crevice, and we entered "Ville de Rouen," a development of a score of high-rise apartment houses, prefabricated and new, some still under construction, and not unlike the *Tours* of the 13e Arrondissement of Paris.

John described the group we would visit:

"Actually there's about fifteen people out there, and every night it's like a big party. One man throws a dinner at his house, and you go over to the other man's house for whisky and pop music. And they shift every night, so every person gets hit every fifteen days, you see. They all work together."

Had he ever been there when they had a political discussion?

"Oh, yes. I've been there when their Communist Party got together. They invited me in just like I was a member. They don't mind speaking in front of me. If I didn't understand something, I'd say, 'Wait a minute,' and they'd explain it to me. They're very, very beautiful. I was told that there are fifteen beds in Rouen where I can stay, and anytime I feel like coming out, I can bring anyone along with me I like.

"Everytime I come, we go out for a big dinner, and they insist on paying for everything. If I get there on a Sunday night, and they have to go to work on a Monday morning, they just leave a key on the coffee table—they don't even wake me up—and they always leave some money just in case I don't have any. They're terrific people, they really are."

I don't know why that led me to expect a clan of jolly, sun-baked sixty-year-olds, but when twenty minutes later we entered a modern, colorful apartment and a gathering of exuberant, modish young couples began to form to celebrate John's arrival, I was surprised. We were in the apartment of

Gérard Héliot, a young sociologist at the Rouen School of Architecture, and of his vibrant Spanish wife whose name was, appropriately, Liberté. It was the apartment where John had first been brought by Luc Cloche, who was one of Gérard's students. Gérard was quickly on the phone to Annette Lanoix, the professor of English at the university, just as he had been that night in September 1969. She was our translator, and she arrived shortly with her husband, Louis, who commutes to Paris every week to teach English at a *lycée*.

Over a meal of pâté, meat, white wine, and camembert, which Liberté called *"fromage* for men" and John would not touch, they told their side of John's appearance in their midst. They didn't know quite what to do at first, Annette explained. They'd all talked about the American deserter situation, and approved of desertion unanimously in their disgust over American policy. But when a deserter arrived in the flesh, it became a different matter. They needed to find out whether or not he was an impostor. One had to be careful, she said, because there had been reports of people who posed as deserters. So they had a small meal before the interrogation, all, she said, feeling "a bit awkward." They cross-examined John for over an hour, and made up their minds that he was genuine, that although his act had not been motivated politically, it did have political meaning. And then they had a big meal to celebrate the occasion.

The caution had been maintained for the two days that followed. Things were not very secure and stable at the time, Annette said. It was difficult to find names and addresses of people or organizations who might help. "We knew that the S.D.S. had been infiltrated by the CIA," she said. "There was the danger, we thought, that John might be handed over to the Americans. And so we decided that the Quakers were the safest." This call was made, and the Quakers agreed to take John as long as he didn't take drugs.

I asked them what their politics were. Gérard Héliot described himself as extreme left, but he did not belong to the Communist Party, he said. Luc Cloche was described as a Trotskyist and later Communist. But while there was a display of labels and the rhetoric of radicalism, I got no impression that these young, hip intellectuals were plotting to overthrow the government of Rouen by force and violence, and while they were interested in John's situation for its political content, they appeared to like him genuinely and had clearly been kind to him in a very human way.

Gérard and I then went down into Rouen to get Kallisher. I wanted to explain to Kallisher the significance of John's case, because I was skeptical that old-hand foreign correspondents were abreast of the growing debate on amnesty in the country, a debate which had only developed in the preceding few months. Jon Randal had asked me the day before to brief him on the elements of the debate, because he said he had been out of the country for all purposes since 1953. Peter Kallisher's situation was not dissimilar, and he had also been a correspondent in Vietnam. For all I knew he might have been fascinated by the brigandage of it.

When we arrived back at Ville de Rouen, I told Kallisher that I would have to advise John on any interview that might be held. This, Kallisher objected to vehemently, saying they did not even allow Pompidou that kind of privilege of censorship, and that if it happened he would have to tell his bosses in New York. I had seen little people who are unequipped with the defenses of public officials backed into corners by newsmen too often in my career. I had done it myself. I said I was sorry, but John faced criminal charges when he arrived home, and anything he said on national TV could be held against him. Kallisher continued to object. "Coach him all you like," he said, "but no censorship."

We left it that the shooting that evening would simply be "ambiance," and we'd talk about the interview later.

The idea of "ambiance" under the glare of lights, whirring cameras, the "Cuts," "Start Agains," the changes of reel, the long lens stuck under one's chin, and the microphone under the pillow was something of a joke. But John seemed remarkably calm and adept through it all. The ambiance took a political tack, sometimes far out of John's frame of reference, but some interesting things were said.

"Is anybody going to be forgiven for the Vietnam War?" Louis Lanoix asked.

John mentioned Calley. "If President Nixon can free him, after he killed 102, why should he prosecute me, since I've been there and refused to go back?"

"That's your problem," Louis replied.

"No, that's his problem," John said.

"But if they set you free, then the war can't go on, because nobody will want to go."

"This is what I hope will happen. I'm hoping that we can get a universal amnesty, and that this will put a complete end to the Vietnam War," John said.

It was the perfect answer to the anti-war critics, including resisters in exile, who claimed that the amnesty diverted people's attention from the cause of ending the war. Amnesty and anti-war protest are wedded; they are based together in the realization of American war crimes; together they urge responsibility for these crimes at the highest levels. Thus, pressure for amnesty can only hasten the end of the war. But Kallisher was displeased. "It's too political. Talk about hamburgers or . . ."

"What's political about a hamburger?" Louis objected.

But the tone of the conversation switched, and Kallisher got what he wanted: that the first thing John wanted to eat when he arrived home was a cheeseburger and a glass of chocolate milk, and that he greatly looked forward to getting back to his motorcycle.

"What will you miss the most?" Louis asked.

"My friends here in France," John replied.

It was over; John had been asked questions as tough as anyone could ask him and had done beautifully. I told Kallisher I'd changed my mind—John could handle the interview on his own.

I turned to Joe Masraff, the cameraman, and asked him what he thought.

"He's not the right guy," he said. It was the first of several times I was to hear that remark. What was he looking for? What are all Americans looking for as a model for amnesty? Do they require for forgiveness someone with a haircut like McGeorge Bundy, or with the articulateness of Rhodes Scholar Rusk, or someone with the military acumen of Maxwell Taylor, or the experience in public affairs of Richard

Nixon: a demeanor like all those men who, we have been told, are the only ones in a position to make the moral decisions of public policy? What does America want to believe about those who have left her over Vietnam?

"He's not sexy enough." He shook his head.

John and I left about 2 A.M.—I was pretty drunk on cognac—and returned to the hotel. He told me the next morning that he had stood in the shower for over a half hour after we had parted. It was the first shower he'd had in eight months.

★ SATURDAY, MARCH 18, 1972 ★

I had slept well for the first and only night in France, even if it was short. John knocked on my door at 7 A.M., dressed, showered, and alert. I told him to come back in an hour. At nine o'clock we met the CBS crew at their hotel across from the train station. Joe Masraff appeared to pay the hotel bill with a 500-franc bill which made John's eyes pop. Peter Kallisher arrived and we had a quick coffee. Kallisher commented that he knew people like John's French friends—"They would never take in an American except for who he [John] is and what he is."

John would remember the crack later and say: "No, this is the way these people are."

At 9:30 Louis and Annette Lanoix arrived, and a few minutes later the others. Kallisher had them convene in a café down the street, where they all huddled around John in the chilly, damp morning outside and had hot tea. Kallisher liked the "ambiance." The steam rising off the tea made good television. "Much better than last night," he said.

Then they all walked toward the station with the cameras behind them. (I dutifully stayed out of the picture at Kallisher's request.) In the farewell outside, Louis hammed it up a bit by kissing John on both cheeks (they'd only met the night before), but that was good television too. And then we boarded the 10:15 train for Paris.

On the train, as John talked and I wrote, we sketched out

a rough draft of what he might say to the press at the airport in forty-eight hours.

Tod and Annette were sitting in the vestibule of the hotel
on the Rue des Écoles when we arrived at noon. Tod looked
sleepy—he is a night person—but also worried. "We've had
a little incident," he said. "It's nothing to get too uptight
about, but we've got to be careful now." He told us about
the visit of the police to the H.L.M. on Thursday night. On
Friday afternoon, Annette had finally called Joe Heflin, a
draft resister who had burned his draft card two years before
near Memphis and later announced the action from a pulpit
in a black Methodist Church. Joe, who was to become a
great help to us in these last few days, had gotten hold of
Mike and Tod, and they had met. Joe had been quite agi-
tated.

"Haven't you ever heard of Corsica?" he asked them. The
specter of Corsica—the place where Max had been exiled
after his first kidnapping—was now to become a factor.

Joe was frantic with worry that there might be another
visit to the H.L.M. by the police. They had surely hoped to
find John there. That evening, reluctantly, Joe went over to
Annette's apartment and packed up the books that were
around the place and the copies of Rita Act's newspapers.
The latter he and Annette dumped in a vacant lot. The night
was windy, and scores of Safe Conduct passes through Viet
Cong lines blew helter-skelter down the street.

When the story was over, John turned on Annette. "Why
didn't you tell me?" he snapped at her. She shrugged her
shoulders and looked away.

Mike arrived. At this point he strongly feared deportation
and/or that John or Annette would be picked up and held
for five days. Tod managed to calm him. Talk of deportation
seemed melodramatic to me, despite Maria's stories of Max
and Coryell. Furthermore, Maria had said, "The time is past
when a telephone could be lifted at 4 Avenue Gabriel [CIA]
to communicate to a parallel police their desiderata." And
besides, we were "*messieurs*," who would know what to do,
not "poor flunkies."

Nonetheless, we decided that John and Annette would be

moved into our hotel, and that they were never to go anywhere without one of us along. I registered back into Hôtel
St. Jacques for a room on the top floor, one floor above Tod,
and then went up the street to the Hôtel Claude Bernard
and registered again under the name of Keston.

Then John and I went off to see Jon Randal. When we
arrived at his office on the Rue du Berri, he informed me
that the lawyer, Bourget, had called with an answer from
the Ministry of Interior: Monsieur Canton, the head of the
foreigners' section, had told him that the French government's main concern was that its policy of political asylum be
protected. It must not appear that John was being kicked
out of the country by the French; therefore, Christian believed that if a legal document were drawn up to state that
John had had no difficulties with the French Government,
the French would not object to his departure. Bourget requested that John be brought to his office at 9 A.M. on
Monday on the way to Orly. This news was an enormous
relief to me. Now we could be quite sure that if John were
turned back, the American Embassy would be behind it.

We went off to Randal's favorite bistro, where we all had a
salad that John was to comment on constantly for the next
two days: "It had meat in it, Annette!" Randal interviewed
John.

Later in the afternoon, Kallisher arrived at the hotel, and
John, Annette, and Tod went with the CBS team to the
Place d'Italie where the couple was filmed in their local
market. Annette had vetoed Kallisher's request to film in
their apartment. It would be construed as political work,
she thought.

On the way back on the *métro*, John, well-fed and in good
spirits, sang quietly, "I'm an old cow-hand from the Rio
Grande . . ." At the hotel at 3 P.M. I conveyed Bourget's
information to Mike and Tod. Skepticism gripped them
still, and they were not convinced; I became the optimist.
Nonetheless, the chances of boarding were clearly enhanced,
and it was decided that Mike should fly back to New York
to prepare for John's arrival.

Mike and I went off to the Champs Élysées to buy his

ticket to New York. From the TWA office, he telephoned John Hess of the *New York Times,* and they set up a meeting for a briefing. It was six o'clock, and I rushed off to the Place des Victoires to buy a bikini for my wife before the boutique of Jon Randal's recommendation closed at seven. It had literally been the only free hour in the week that I had found to perform that necessary task, much less have a moment to visit the Louvre.

We convened in John and Annette's room in the Saint Jacques at eight. Tod brought a bottle of wine for them, along with stuffed grape leaves and Boursin cheese. We reminisced some, and John gave a lecture to Annette:

"Keep cool, old lady. Don't let the police fuck over ya. I'll give you an address of a lawyer, and as soon as I hit the States, we're going to try to get a leave." (Tod had indicated that they would try to get a three-day humanitarian leave for John from military custody.) "If I get out of custody, I'll jump down to the Providence Savings Bank, and wire you $1000 into the ITT Bank here, which they turn over to the American Express. You go down and they'll pay you in cash . . . . I'll do that instead of a draft check. If I do it that way, it will take you a month to get it cashed. Move the hell out of the H.L.M. I don't care if you're paying 700 or 800 francs a fuckin' month—and move into a goddamn apartment, and nobody knows where you live. Don't give the address away. You can expect something within five days of when I hit the States. Get a place where you can pay three months at a time. And I'll take care of the rest. When I get over here again, we'll press and go to court, get the kid, and split."

Annette nodded obediently without comment.

Mike left for a deserters' dinner which had become a weekly affair in Paris. Mike did not tell the deserters that night about John's imminent departure. He was too afraid of infiltration.

★ SUNDAY, MARCH 19 ★

At 9:30 I left the Hotel Claude Bernard and went to buy the *Herald Tribune*. The most prominent Vietnam story, displayed in a takeout on the front page, began as follows:

The U.S. Navy has pulled a supersecret team of "warrior porpoises" out of Vietnam after a year of duty in which they guarded against enemy frogmen, military sources said today. . . . The porpoises were deployed in Cam Ranh Bay with weapons attached to their snouts, and on several occasions they killed underwater guerrillas. Although their presence was known throughout the country, the Navy stamped top secret on the project and refused to answer nearly all questions about them.

In other war news, the paper carried a report of a Vietnam troop level of 114,500 as of March 9, 1972.

At the Hotel St. Jacques, I picked up a tray of coffee and croissants and took it to the top floor. That morning and the next, I went through the same routine; I half-expected that John and Annette would not answer when I knocked. Our tricks were, after all, slim protection against a determined police force.

At 10 o'clock a deserter I'll call Luke arrived at the hotel for his appointment with me. He had been one of the people that Mike and Tod had first suggested as a possibility for the test case. John, Annette, and Tod went off with Kallisher to the Bois de Boulogne for Kallisher's much-awaited interviews, and Luke and I settled down to talk. He had a benign round face; his head that day was wrapped in a purple bandana which made him look like a pirate from the Barbary coast. Luke was very cautious, which is clearly the mark of anyone who has survived exile successfully. Much of his story he asked me "as a man" not to tell. What I mainly wanted to know was his reaction to John's return.

Luke had been in exile slightly longer than John. He had been a Marine and had gone through basic training at Camp Pendleton and Advanced Infantry Training and guerilla training as well. After AIT he stated his intention to apply for a CO classification. The Marines put every obstacle in his path and assigned him to special guerilla training. He went AWOL, returning to his home in the East. There his family received a letter which all families of an absent GI receive. There is no form for such a letter but the commander follows the regulation in AR 630-10, *Absence with-*

out Leave and Desertion, section 2-4(e), entitled "Notify next of kin."

e. Notify next of kin. The unit commander will notify the absentee's nearest relative immediately by letter when the member has been absent for 10 days or if it has been determined that the absentee has sought political asylum in, is voluntarily residing in, or is detained by a foreign country. The letter will advise the relative that the individual is absent without leave and the date of the absence; that continued absence may result in conviction for desertion with resultant loss in pay and allowance, confinement, dismissal, and dishonorable or bad conduct discharge; that allotments and allowances may be discontinued; that dependents become ineligible for medical care, commissary privileges or other benefits if the member is dropped as a deserter; and that the absentee be urged to return to military control if his whereabouts is known. Extreme statements such as "life imprisonment" or "death by a firing squad" will not be used.

In Luke's case the Army's psychology worked well. His parents put pressure on him. Luke went to the Deputy Mayor of his city who was the same ethnic origin as he. They talked and the Deputy Mayor wrote a letter confirming the religious basis for Luke's request. With this in hand, he returned to Camp Pendleton and was immediately thrown in jail. The authorities took the letter and it was never mentioned again. Some time later, two sergeants appeared at his cell and had him pack his bags. They took him to an airport and, under the surveillance of a Marine captain, he was taken to a Pacific staging area for Vietnam. In the first few weeks he was there he was taunted. "Go on," they said, "make your break now." There was nowhere to go—they thought. Luke went AWOL *on* the military base. He lived in a different barracks among enlisted Marines who hid him. And then when the chance came he smuggled his way onto a Far Eastern ship and left. He lived for two years underground in the Orient in a country that provides no asylum for deserters. "Legally it was bad," Luke said, "but morally it was good!" He learned the language and delved into the culture. "I don't believe that a soldier should desert just to desert. He must learn from the experience," Luke said. It took him two years to get the passport from the underground that enabled him to come to France.

Luke had been in France five months. He was unemployed. He knew John only slightly but John had tried to help him find a job and he knew of another deserter that John had helped. I asked Luke about John's bumming. He did not know about it, he said, but if it were true, he would think no less of John. "I do not judge," he said. "It's in the Bible."

Mike Uhl had told Luke in private the night before the broad outline of what we were doing with John. I told him specifically what and when (I knew Mike and Tod trusted him) and asked him what he thought about it. His reply was rather detached. It will be interesting to ascertain how the people feel about desertion, he said, to find out how they react to those of us whose "only crime is refusing to commit a crime." He would be watching to see if they made an example of John. "The American government and the American people have got to deal with this problem," he said. "They've got to be de-educated from the propaganda they've been hearing!"

"But," Luke went on to say, "my experience cannot help but make me doubt justice in a military court or any court. When you pass through these experiences, you begin to lose respect for the authorities. You no longer believe in their honor. Soul is sublimated . . . and I'm aware of how slowly the political processes work."

Would he consider being a follow-up if John's case worked out all right? "Perhaps," he replied, "but I'm not sure I'm ready to go back yet."

Luke's fatalism astonished me. His responses were calm and unhurried. He had come to expect little from authorities. It was a quality John had exhibited also, and I believe it flowed in both their cases from the belief that they were right in their actions, and the country would have to come to them. John had said, "I'm very, very pleased to be the first one to come back in this way, not for me, but for exiles in general. But whether I'm first or fifth does not matter. It is something I have to do." And when I asked him if he thought we would go on Monday, he said, "Yeah, I do. But if we don't go Monday, I figure we'll go sometime next week."

Luke and I talked about amnesty, and he continued in his philosophical vein revealing his concern for the brotherhood of exile.

"If you can't get total amnesty, there might be other people who would want two years alternative service—not me, but others. If you can't get all the cake, it might be good for some to get part. I don't think it would be just, objectively or morally, but I wouldn't prevent others from having it if that is what they want."

And then he said, "A man comes into this world, and he's entitled to his life."

Tod and John came back chortling about the Kallisher interview. He'd been asked the same old questions, John said, and he was getting pretty good at the answers. But at one point they had gotten into what had made John decide to go back.

JH: "I'm not French to begin with. France is not my country. Therefore, my struggle is in America, not in France. I want to go back to the root of the problem and start there."

PK: "Are you talking about a personal or political problem?"

JH: "I'm talking about the problem that the United States has today of the number of people they have in exile. Now the country has to come up with a plan to get these people to come back, to let them come back. . . . I don't mean forgiveness, because I don't think these people need to be forgiven, because they have committed no crimes whatsoever."

PK: "According to the laws of the United States as they exist today, they have."

JH: "That's according to the laws of the United States to-day, but why would a country like the United States prosecute a man for what he thinks is right? Correct?

Did he do something wrong to be forgiven? I think the country would be lucky if he forgives them."

PK: (in good, objective, journalistic fashion): "O.K., that's your point of view."

John, Annette, and I caught the *métro* for Nationale. It was John's last trip to the apartment where they had lived for nearly a year. He continued in his buoyant mood, caressing Annette often, telling me how she had been known as "Snookey" to him, and he "Poopsey" to her, which made quite a family with Snuggles the cat. And John sang and giggled along the way, "If you want to be mine, just pull the twine. Ah hold my pants up with a piece of twine." And later, "Lost my last quarter in a rubber machine. . ."

"Well, old girl," he said, "I'll have you in the States before long—just a matter of time. You want to live in my house in America?"

"Yeah," she replied.

"The thing about marriage in the United States," he said, "it takes about three days. Over here it takes about a month." And he went on with a fantasy about a $40,000 house overlooking the Chesapeake Bay in Annapolis.

Annette told him he should look like a clean-cut innocent guy the next day. "That mustache makes you look like a killer," she joked at him.

It was playful tender stuff which appealed to my sentimental side. John said of those last few days, "We had quite a few arguments in the time we lived together, but the last couple of days were really, really beautiful. We could really relate to one another, really get down and do some serious talking. She didn't understand what was happening. There were times when none of us were on top of it. But she had to know what was going on. She was involved. So I had long talks with her about it, tried to break it down and explain it to her. It was nice . . . a nice moment . . . just like somebody reaching for a memory to hold for the rest of their life. Of course, we realized that it was too late. I believe at that period, Annette and I were the closest we'd ever been, outside of when we first started living together."

At the apartment there was a scene about the books that Joe Heflin had removed on Friday. John was most concerned about his foreign coin and bill collection, but he found the bills in an atlas that Joe had left, including a huge Russian bill from the 1890s, which he said was worth $5550, and some Brazilian bills. The latter had more significance than as a collector's item. "Whenever the police would stop me and ask if I had any money, I used to pull out the Brazilian bills. They'd say, 'Oh, O.K., go ahead.' The bills aren't any good anyway. They're out of date."

The main purpose of this trip was to remove the *Tricontinentals*, Czechoslovakian magazines, and something else called *For Peace Through Individual Freedom*, printed in Havana. John said it was illegal to have them and could cause Annette trouble. Not one looked as if it had been read. Going through his papers, John found a letter from Max which he showed me. Part of it said:

> Dear John,
> Have wanted to write you sometime now, but we are so busy with the GIs here. Yesterday we were in Mainz, not with the 509th but with two Americans, young preachers (well they studied religion but you wouldn't know it to look at them). We turned them on to GI work. Made them FRITAS (friends of Ritas, resisters inside the army) They now go down to Camp Pieri, don't know if you know it, in Wiesbaden and help the GIs there get their shit together. The GIs can decide what they want to do but there's a lot that a civilian can do to help them, if he knows how to talk to them. They are going to the stockade soon, to visit the ritas inside. Things have been blowing up all over! Do you know what some guys have been doing here? They put some rubber bands around a grenade (must be a pretty small one, in my days they were too big to go into the tank hole) pull the pin (damn careful that the rubber bands don't slip off, nor let the handle go), then put it into the C.O.'s (a bastard) jeep's gas tank. The gas eats through the rubber, then bang. What won't people think of next. In this case some stoolie (maybe the guy who did it with them) squealed

and they found the grenade before it went off, but it really pissed off the C.O.

It seemed like an odd style for a forty-four-year-old Austrian professor of geophysics.

I left them at five at the hotel with Tod and John Hess of the *New York Times* and went off for a walk. Feeling dizzy and tense I wandered off in a daze and ended up listening for an hour to a thundering organ recital in the sublime setting of Notre Dame. After a meal on the Quai de la Tournée, I returned to the hotel at 9:30 and, according to plan, began to leak the story to the French and American newspapers that we had not covered. A correspondent from L'Express said he would like to be there. "It might be fun," he said. But he had to go to England in the morning. He gave me another name on the paper. Another writer, an editor from *France Soir*, said he would he a reporter there, but that he doubted we would board.

At 10:15 John, Annette, and Tod came to my room. We worked on the statement. When I had something typed, I handed it to John. He read it aloud—haltingly, torturously slow and inept. I worked at yanking out the big words and the long sentences: "restoration of civil rights and benefits," "repatriation without strings." We changed his thanks to the French government for "providing aid and comfort"— too much like "aid and comfort to the enemy"—to "support and help." John read it again. It was no better. I suggested that we just type the thing up and hand it out at the airport. "No," Tod said, "he'll just have to practice." John said he'd read poorly because he was so tired.

We checked out our schedules and contingencies for the morning and then walked to the other hotel. I accompanied John and Annette to their room.

"Have a good night—not necessarily a good sleep," I said. They did.

★ MONDAY, MARCH 20, 1972 ★

"May I speak to the duty officer, please."
It was 7:30 A.M. and the operation was on! I was given the

home number of John Trattner, who is a press attaché at the Embassy. I gave him the facts: an American deserter without passport or military leave papers would be trying to board TWA's Flight 803 at noon; he was refusing to return under the aegis of the Embassy; CBS news and other press would be at the airport; I was writing a book about the case; and did the Embassy intend to let him board?

There was some wrestling around for facts, talk about immigration regulations, something about the man who handles these matters being out of town. I replied that the deserter was under the sponsorship of a group who did not intend to let this be a matter for French immigration, and that they placed full responsibility for the decision of boarding on the American Embassy. He gave me the name of a female consular official and told me to call back after nine o'clock. I called her.

"He doesn't have a passport?" she said.

"No."

"Then I suppose he can't board."

I used CBS again: "I can assure you that if he isn't boarded, they will all jump in a car and come to the Embassy to ask why, with cameras rolling."

She said she would have to make some calls.

I checked out of the Claude Bernard and walked down to the Hôtel St. Jacques. John and Annette were ready when I brought them their breakfast. John was standing out on the balcony looking across rooftops to the towers of Notre Dame. Annette said he'd practiced his statement to the City of Paris for an hour that morning from the balcony. Tod arrived. We checked out and walked down to the Boulevard St.-Germain des Près. They caught a cab for Christian Bourget's office in Raspail. I stayed behind to call the Associated Press. Then I tried to catch a cab for the air terminal at Invalides. Few were around. One that stopped refused to take me across town through the heavy morning traffic. So I lugged my suitcase down into the *métro*. It was in the spirit of the week. We had been dealing on the highest political level and taking *métros*. I felt as if I had spent more time underground the last few days than above.

At nine o'clock, Tod, Annette, and John were ushered into Bourget's office of Bourget, where his partner Bernard Villette was waiting. He called French immigration and took down the form for a statement from the person on the other end. Shortly thereafter, a notarized affidavit from John to French immigration authorities was drawn up stating that John was not leaving France under any duress or coercion, but rather of his own free will. Shortly after that, Jon Randal arrived. He called the Embassy for their position on the Herndon case. Tod was getting nervous as the minutes passed, but then the arrangements were set, and they left. Christian Bourget met them on the street on the way out and they all piled in Jon Randal's car.

At 9:15 I called Trattner from Invalides. He was out of the office. I asked his secretary if the Embassy had a "Captain Friedberg" in the military attaché's office. She confirmed that there was a Captain John C. Fredenberger there. She transferred me to him. I explained to him who I was—as if he didn't know—and asked if he knew John Herndon. He did and confirmed that they had met earlier in the month. What had they discussed? I asked. "You'll have to get that from Herndon," he replied. I said that I had it from Herndon already that he, Fredenberger, and a CIA man, had tried to buy Herndon off with 300 francs. Fredenberger replied he had no comment, other than to state that what had transpired between Herndon and himself had been a "confidential legal matter."

It was 9:27. The bus left for Orly at 9:30. I hung up and rushed downstairs. Too late. The bus was full, and the glass doors to the bus platform closed tight. I beat on the glass, but got no response. Another man came along who was in the same predicament. We shared a cab together to the airport. He turned out to be an English yoga instructor.

The establishment and leftist press were waiting at the airport when I arrived at ten, and the TV cameras were already set up. I went immediately to TWA and asked a woman who seemed to be in charge if she knew what all the fuss was about. "Something about a deserter," she said. I identified myself as a member of the group who was sponsoring his return. She put me through on the telephone to a

TWA executive downtown, and I explained the situation to him. "TWA is not involved," I insisted. "This is a political matter. Herndon is ticketed and will use his military ID card as documentation. French immigration is abreast of the situation." He thanked me for informing him.

The others arrived at 10:10. I conferred with Tod, relaying confirmation of John's meeting with Fredenberger earlier in the month. Bourget huddled with French immigration and police. The press gathered, and John stepped in front of the cameras. We were determined not to act as if there was any doubt that we would board.

"First of all," John began, "as I leave France now after two-and-a-half years in exile here, I want to thank the French people for providing me support and help during my stay here in France.

"I am, however, an American citizen and a Vietnam veteran. I want to go home to America because my struggle is there, not in France. What happens to me will have strong bearing on what happens to the exile community in general. I am not going back asking the country for forgiveness. I have done what I think is right. That has been refusing to· participate further in the war in Vietnam. I was in Vietnam. I was wounded in Vietnam. I refused to go back a second time after I had been there fifteen months. I would go back to Vietnam voluntarily, if there were some way I could help the people without killing the people.

"I ask the American people to grant universal amnesty for people like me opposed to the war in Vietnam who are now in exile. By universal amnesty, I mean being able to go back to the United States without fear of being prosecuted and by restoring full rights and benefits.

"I believe I will be speaking for the majority of the 'self-retired' veterans who are not here to speak for themselves. They will return to America only with unconditional amnesty. I know from having lived in forced exile for over two years that this is a high enough price to pay for what I believe. I believe that the vast majority of the active duty personnel are opposed to the war in Vietnam and have respect for those of us who have refused to participate.

"It's time for the country to do something for its younger

generation. We have done something for it. I went to Vietnam for it. We've done our share. Now the country can do its."

He enunciated the statement clearly, without mistake, pacing himself almost professionally, speaking with conviction to the cameras and to the American people beyond them, and referring only occasionally to the now-crumpled piece of paper that he held, unshaking, before him. He had indeed mastered the statement that morning, and he was rested. I was quite amazed.

Tod Ensign then stepped forward, identifying himself as John's attorney, and a representative of the Safe Return committee, "a group of Americans concerned about the question of Vietnam, and about the thousands and thousands of men who have deserted, gone underground, or resisted the draft."

"John's going back with us today to New York. We're going to be surrendering to military authorities there, and John will be taking his case into the courts to fight the Army's charges of desertion. We feel that, when John refused to go back to Vietnam from Germany two years ago, this was his duty, not something for which he should now be punished. He had a responsibility to not go back to Vietnam, given the policies of the United States Government in Indochina. We support John, and we hope that his will be the first of several cases of men returning to fight openly for full and complete universal amnesty without any conditions whatsoever."

"What's the position of the American Embassy here on this?" Kallisher asked.

"The American Embassy was contacted here this morning. Captain Fredenberger, who's the military attaché with the Embassy, indicated that he had met with John a couple of weeks ago at which time he told John that he would allow him to return to the United States only under the U.S. Embassy's control and surveillance. John—I think I can speak for him—has had enough of U.S. benevolence as a soldier and as man in Vietnam, and he wants to return under his own power.

"One other point, they have denied John a passport, which makes it even more difficult for us to see that he's boarded here today."

Tod kicked himself later. He had intended to end by saying: "And we do intend to abide by the two-drink limit on the flight." Joe Masraff would have liked that reference to Ambassador Watson.

We then moved to the TWA counter. Christian Bourget informed us that the French would pass John through. He would be boarded! There was a great deal of congratulations but the most enthusiastic came from Joe Heflin, who would be left behind in exile. He was slapping hands and backs all around. Tod pulled out his TWA "Getaway" Card and paid for his and John's ticket with it. John presented a battered military ID card whose lamination was so cracked that it hung limp like cloth. The cameras caught the whole scene. I went off to call the Embassy again.

When I told Trattner that the French were going to board John, he finally stated the Embassy's position. He explained blandly that Herndon's was a routine citizenship case. His military ID card was not enough to establish citizenship, he said, since American citizenship is not required to enlist in the American Army. If the French had not boarded Herndon, he said, two options were available: (1) he could have put himself under military control, whereupon he would have been provided military documentation and a plane ticket, or (2) wholly apart from military control, the Embassy would have provided him documentation for a return trip, and *he* would have been responsible for the ticket. Finally, Trattner said, there had been no contact between French and American officials on the Herndon affair that morning.

I returned to the ticket counter to find a new crisis. TWA was putting up objections to John's boarding. What right did they have! It made me furious, when we were this close. Tod explained that the company had agreements on documentation with the French government. He was calm about it, and the flap was soon over. TWA was simply making a show of how seriously they took their arrangements with the French. We were soon on our way to the boarding area. Outside customs John and Annette kissed passionately— and publicly, in front of the cameras—and then he was skirted through customs, since he was taking home only the clothes on his back. The plainclothesmen with him called Tod through customs also. They were evidently afraid that after all the trouble John would slip back out and bolt for Paris. When John heard what the trouble was, he said to one of the policemen:

"Christ, man, it took me four days to get on this flight. You think I want to desert back to Paris now?"

For Tod and me, the taxi and takeoff of Flight 803 was the end of a long and torturous episode which had had a happy end. We were boarded, and in a way that would dramatize the issue of amnesty. What a victory! There was little sense that a more important episode was about to begin. As the stewardness served us drinks, we reminisced about the week as if we were teenagers on a school bus, riding home after a baseball triumph over the chief rival. John shared in our joy, but his thoughts were mixed with sorrow.

"What hurt was when that plane started to take off from that runway.... That hurt, because then I knew I had to leave her behind and go. And I'll bet you Annette went home and cried. I know she did. I know that for a fact, and I wasn't even there."

The illusion of victory lasted for several hours. When the shades went down for the canned movie—some awful *ménage à trois*—I went to sleep for a few hours.

Two hours out of New York, John and I huddled to discuss an airport statement at JFK. John was clearly looking forward to it now. He had done so well in Paris that we decided to simply make up a list of topics for him to refer to: VIETNAM VET AND CASUALTY . . . 2½ YEARS FORCED EXILE . . . HIGH PRICE . . . NO FORGIVENESS . . . UNIVERSAL AMNESTY. We agreed that he had not stressed enough in Paris the high price of forced exile.

When we began to descend, I looked out to see Nantucket and pointed it out to John, leaning over him as he sat in the window seat. Over Martha's Vineyard I pointed out Chappaquiddick and the Vineyard Sound.

"It looks like a nice place to go fishing," he said. I said it was.

Past Block Island, descending into reality; then over Montauk Point, I must have glanced at him unconsciously.

"You looked at me like you was worried or something, wantin' to see if I was looking worried too," he said. I did not know my face conveyed my feelings that easily.

On the ramp a six-foot first lieutenant in the Army stepped in front of John. Behind the officer were four enlisted MPs: a Marine, a Coast Guard sailor, an Air Force man, and an Army man. It seemed to indicate that this was a Pentagon-level arrest.

"John David Herndon?"

"Yes."

"I will read to you your rights under Article 32 of the Uniform Code of Military Justice . . . ."

★GREETINGS★

Now his elder son was in the field: and as he came and drew nigh to the house, he heard musick and dancing.

And he called one of the servants and asked what these things meant.

And he said unto him, thy brother is come; and thy father hath killed the fatted calf, because he hath received him safe and sound.

And he was angry, and would not go in: therefore came his father out, and entreated him.

And he answering said to his father, Lo these many years do I serve thee, neither transgressed I at any time thy commandment: and yet thou never gavest me a kid, that I might make merry with my friends:

But as soon as this thy son was come, which hath devoured thy living with harlots, thou hast killed for him the fatted calf.

And he said unto him, Son, thou art ever with me, and all I have is thine.

It was meet that we should make merry, and be glad: for this thy brother was dead, and is alive again; and was lost and is found.

Luke, Chapter 15 ed.: 25–32

vocative words have been used with great frequency in the American withdrawal from Vietnam, but none more frequently than "peace with honor." This has led the adversaries of the Nixon Administration to rebut with the concept of "peace with dignity" implying that a faster withdrawal would be more dignified. And so we are mired down in these concepts. But whatever concept is the goal, the reality is that the United States has not withdrawn its forces very gracefully from Vietnam. In fact, revenge has characterized that withdrawal, the lashing out of a blinded, furious Cyclops, hurling its mines and bombs about, but Ulysses is already safely away, having slipped out of the giant's reach hidden under the belly of sheep.

The question is whether in the postwar period the giant will continue to lash out. Will vindictiveness or generosity distinguish that period? Will the country be able to rise from its moral collapse? The reception of John David Herndon is a glimpse into the future. It indicates how the government may attempt to react on the question of loyalty and how it can be made to react. The reaction to the Herndon case by ordinary American indicates how fundamentally amnesty challenges their deep beliefs, and how those beliefs must alter if we, as a people and a nation, are to learn from the Vietnam experience. Thus, John's case has wide implications, and not the least, for John himself

On Sunday evening, March 19, Mr. and Mrs. James Herndon received a call from Mike Uhl in their Baltimore home, telling them of John's probable arrival the next morning, and asking them if they could be at Kennedy airport at one P.M. The conversation was quick and not altogether communicative because the Herndons were left with the impression that by some miracle they would be able to pick up their son at the airport and bring him home.

When they arrived at the TWA terminal the next day, a half-hour before the expected arrival, a TV camera crew was setting up, and the Herndons were confused, wondering what celebrity might be expected. As one of the many ironies of the Herndon affair, President Nixon happened to be visiting Kennedy that day, inspecting new customs facilities at a different part of the airport. But then a "nice, handsome young man" came over and introduced himself as Steve Young of CBS News. Young explained the situation and the Herndons' misapprehension was cleared up quickly. And then a tall thin "hippie-looking" fellow in jeans started towards them, and Mrs. Herndon whispered to her husband. "That's gotta be Mike."

Behind the customs barriers out of sight of the cameras the military was preparing its getaway. Their information was that the press, including French journalists, was on the plane with Herndon. A military press officer was there to handle them. A military helicopter had been flown in to facilitate a quick escape if it was needed. A small room on the side of the TWA customs area was made available.

When John was taken into custody, he was escorted briskly to this small room, with Tod along as his lawyer. (I was forced to go through normal customs and not allowed into the room.) There John was strip-searched. The explanation given for this search was that the military wanted to be sure that he had "brought no drugs in with him." He was given fifteen minutes with his parents, skirted out a back door into a car, and driven off. Tod inferred that the Army was prepared to move quickly on the case, but he had no idea how quickly. John was driven to the Brooklyn Navy Yard, and then on to the First Precinct in Manhattan where all

AWOLs are initially taken if they are turned over to the authorities in New York. He spent his first night back in the States there.

On Tuesday morning Tod telephoned the Provost Marshal at the Navy Yard to make an appointment with his client for the afternoon. The lieutenant on the other end made the appointment, without indicating that John was at the First Precinct in Manhattan and neglecting to mention that orders had already been cut at the Continental Army Command (CONARC) headquarters in the Pentagon to have John transferred to Fort Jackson, S.C., that very day. The explanation for this move given later was that twenty military bases around the country handled cases of Herndon's type on a rotation basis, and it was simply Fort Jackson's turn. But the more plausible explanation is that shipping Herndon to Fort Jackson would put him beyond the effective reach of his lawyers and of the support and pressure that Safe Return could exercise.

On Tuesday, Steve Young badgered the Army public information officer about its plans for Herndon. The Colonel put him off; "This old machine doesn't work too fast," he said. But in midafternoon, with Tod about to start off to visit John at the Navy Yard, Young called the Army press office again, and was informed that Herndon was on his way to Newark Airport where he would board a flight to Columbia, S.C. The old machine had evidently acquired a new life. Young called Tod, who immediately rushed to District Court in Brooklyn with Hal Weiner, another lawyer who had handled a number of military defenses in the past, and who would handle John's court-martial. There they filed for a temporary restraining order on the Army pending a hearing to obtain a writ of habeas corpus. The petition alleged that the Army had breached its enlistment contract with Private John Herndon when it required him to violate the International Rules of War as enumerated in the Nuremberg Trials. The petition further alleged that the Army was attempting to frustrate the efforts of his chosen civilian counsel to defend him.

Meanwhile, Mike was on the phone to sympathetic senators and representatives, press, and anti-war activists. Senator Gravel of Alaska met with Colonel Everett O. Post, the Army Senate Liaison. Congresswoman Bella Abzug and Congressman Perrin Mitchell became involved. They, together with Bishop Paul Moore of New York, exerted considerable pressure on the Army. In Brooklyn District Court, the lawyers were unable to obtain a restraining order, but Judge Jacob Mishler did schedule a hearing on Friday, March 24, and recommended that Herndon be kept in the district for the hearing. Colonel Post informed Senator Gravel that Herndon would be kept in New York until the hearing. When John's escort, a captain, called his commander from Newark Airport before boarding the flight to South Carolina, he was ordered to bring John back to Fort Hamilton in Brooklyn.

Tod and Hal Weiner met with John the next morning, March 22. Mike meanwhile learned that contrary to Colonel Post's assurances to Senator Gravel, the Army still planned to ship John to Fort Jackson that afternoon. If the Court ordered it, the Army was prepared to fly him back to New York from South Carolina. This information was confirmed by the Judge Advocate at Fort Hamilton who told the lawyers that the Army would do with Herndon what it "damned well pleased." Mike was back on the phone to Congressional contacts. Senator Gravel personally called the Safe Return office to confer on strategy and began to take more aggressive action, not simply to keep Herndon in New York until Friday, but to amend his orders from Fort Jackson to Fort Dix, New Jersey. Gravel's intervention elevated the case to the Secretary of the Army's desk. On Wednesday afternoon the Army offered Fort Dix as a change of station if Safe Return would relax the pressure. Acceptance of that offer would have meant a cancelation of the Friday hearing in Brooklyn, since Fort Dix is in a different court jurisdiction. Safe Return countered with the demand that the Army deal with Herndon's supporters in open court, presenting amended, written orders to the effect that Herndon would be transferred to Fort Dix for the length of the legal process against him. This the Army agreed to do.

On Friday, the hearing in District Court was a pro forma affair in which the agreement to transfer Herndon to Fort Dix was consummated, and a change of venue for the habeas corpus hearing to District Court in Trenton was approved. Indeed, it was finished so quickly that John's military escort prepared to take the prisoner away, before Congresswoman Bella Abzug could arrive to confer the significance of her presence on the event. Tod and Hal Weiner therefore stalled for as long as they could, pulling papers out of briefcases and appearing to re-explain them laboriously to their client. But finally Bella arrived, and Mike, who had been waiting nervously outside for her, quickly guided her to the State Attorney's office. When the door opened, there was John, shackled to an MP. But Bella turned away from the door to politic with someone behind her, and the door closed for a moment in the confusion. When it opened again and Bella entered the office, John's hands were magically free.

Abzug interviewed John, asking him questions about universal amnesty, how many people he thought were out of the country, how he felt about the war, and why he had left the Army. The interview did not last long. The press was waiting outside the courthouse. Bella introduced John's parents and then said, "We can still salvage many of these men whom we sent to fight an illegal and immoral war." She announced that she would soon introduce a bill for universal amnesty that would "cover men like John Herndon and others who have suffered from their refusal to participate in the war."

Finally, Hal Weiner defined the strategy of his defense of John in court as two-pronged. First, the defense maintained that the Army had no jurisdiction over Herndon since he was given a bad conduct discharge and never notified of its withdrawal. Second, he said, "The Army breached its enlistment contract with him. You can't contract to commit crimes. It's impossible to contract to commit a crime. The Army, by violating its own rules of land warfare, by not distinguishing between combatants and noncombatants, violates laws and treaties of the United States, including treaties in accord with the Geneva Convention, and is doing exactly the thing that they tried people for in Nuremburg. Under the Nuremburg charters, it's his obligation to not do these things as an individual."

After Weiner's statement to the press, John was led off in front of the cameras handcuffed to a thin enlisted MP who, John said, "was shaking so much, I thought he was going to faint right there."

The story of the hearing and Abzug's comments appeared on page 2 of the *Washington Post* the following day along with the Pentagon's reaction. Herndon, according to the Pentagon, was the "type of person" likely to desert for reasons other than moral or political. A military spokesman asserted that John's previous court-martials were for AWOLs, leaving the impression that Herndon was simply a seedy character with a long line of previous offenses. No one objected, strangely, to the Pentagon making this kind of moral judgment. Furthermore, the Pentagon spokesman said, "Inquiries made by field commands and research teams reveal that relatively few soldiers claim the Vietnam war as a motivating factor for desertion. The major causes of desertion, true today as they were in previous wars, are personal problems and the inability to adjust to regimented life." This statement ignored the fact that in each successive year of the Vietnam conflict since 1967, the number of deserters has leapt by the tens of thousands: in 1967, roughly 44,000; in 1968, 54,000; in 1969, 70,000; in 1970, 84,000; in 1971, nearly 100,000. The 1971 figure meant that 177 soldiers out of every thousand in the Army deserted in that year. There is a striking comparison with the figures for 1942–45, when 25,444 were listed as deserters, and the 18,460 listed for the four-year period of the Korean War, 1950–54. Could it be that soldiers in the Vietnam era had so many more "personal" problems?

"Herndon's records," the Pentagon pressed on, "do not reflect that he was wounded in Vietnam or that he had been ordered to Vietnam for a second tour [John had heard he was on levy for Vietnam, which precedes official orders] or that he had reenlisted for duty in the Special Forces." But the Pentagon did not tell the *Washington Post* that Herndon's medical records presented in District Court only went back to 1969, starting a year after John had returned from Vietnam, that his personnel file made no mention of the medals such as the Air Medal and the Army Commendation Medal that he had won in the war zone, even though John has copies of the award certificates himself, and that generally his records, full of erasures and penciled-out entries, looked as if they had been rummaged through by a four-year-old.

In reply to the Army's attempt to dismiss John as a bad character, otherwise stated as the "bafflement" of the Pentagon as to why he had been chosen as the test case, Mike Uhl was quoted in the story as saying, "We're not a bunch of directors from Hollywood. We can't go down to central casting and find the guy who's going to be the typical stereotype guy for this kind of case. He is the first Vietnam veteran, self-retired veteran, who has come back to fight this in a way that will not deny the moral and political nature of his action in the first place."

John passed the following two weeks in a maximum security D cell, Code 1, classified as a "potential trouble-maker." He was allowed one hour a day for recreation during which time he was permitted to fraternize with other prisoners in that cell block. They included an Air Force deserter who had come back quietly, under Embassy guidance, and who had subsequently been charged with desertion and was in pre-trial confinement before a general court-martial. For the rest of the time, John was segregated. His cell was checked every hour at first, and then every half-hour, twenty-four hours a day. And he played the role of the trouble-maker to the hilt.

Once a guard said, "Don't you want to buff the floor?"

"What for?" John replied. "I'm not gettin paid for it. Find somebody who's on a pay status."

Another time, someone ordered him to cut off his mustache.

"I ain't gonna do it. I'm a civilian," he said and made them furious. It is not inconceiveable that John's belligerent behavior in the stockade contributed to the Pentagon's final decision in his case.

Yet another time, John said to a captain who was over his immediate guards,

"Hey, man, why don't you let me out there with the other prisoners?"

"Can't let you do it," the captain had replied.

"Why?"

" 'Cause you're a political prisoner. We got a lot of people around here don't have a high school education. You seem to be pretty smart. You get along fine with all the prisoners. Now I'm not saying something would happen out there. I'm saying something could happen out there."

But John's relationship with his enlisted guards was far from hostile. They kept track of his story in the newspapers and saved clippings for him. One guard would occasionally come rushing in excitedly, "Hey, Herndon, you hit the papers again."

And when Safe Return held a demonstration of 100 people at Fort Dix on April 1, unfurled a large sheet with FREE JOHN HERNDON emblazoned across it, and passed out leaflets with a picture of John shackled between two MPs, John heard all about it from his guards.

In John's second week in the United States an evidence-gathering hearing on his case was held at Fort Dix. Tod Ensign attended the affair. The hearing raised the hope that the Army might act administratively rather than judicially in the case. The authorities seemed to be questioning whether General Almquist had made a mistake in disapproving John's bad conduct discharge in 1970. Tod was suspicious that the tone of the procedure was a ploy.

In this week John wrote me a letter.

April 3, 1972

Dear Jim,

I got your letter yesterday. It is very nice to here from you again.

Well, Jim, right now I'm in a D-Cell that is 5 by 8 by 10 and a lot of time to think. I still feel the same way as I did in Paris only more so now. Because I'm really doing something. Now if everything goes OK I will be out of here in 2 or 3 weeks. . . .

Did you write my wife. If so what did she say? When a good thought comes up I will write it down for you.

Well Give the Power to the People and the States will change.

Right on Brother
John

P.S. I do miss Annette very much. I love her.

[Second sheet:]

Dear Jim,

Well, as I sit here talking to another brother I kind of think of all the fun I had in France and of Annette a lot.

But last night I had a dream and it took place in Rouen. Boy, did we have fun there. In some ways I'm sorry I left and in others I'm glade [sic] I did.

I just can't wait until I get back to Annette. Most of the People over here I can't talk with because they seem like they are 10 years behind me for some reason.

Or is it that I have learned so much about life in the last 3 years. And I know what they are just now learning.

The US will be a good place when we get it the way we want it.

Power,
John.

But John would have to bear his ordeal alone. The line of support to Annette had been broken, and he was lonely and full of doubt in his cell. Annette did not write him for three months, but she did write me three weeks after we had left Paris.

Dear Jim,

I am sorry that I was not honest with you when you came to see John here in Paris. Before I met John I was able to save money. I was never behind in my wash even though I did everything by hand. I was paying 270 F a month rent and making 700 F a month.

Really I was glad to see John go, because I wanted to get rid of him. I have never loved John, but when John first came to live with me, I thought I could learn to love him. Not long after he moved in with me, he found a job and I thought we could lead a good life together, but John lost his job, and he started going down hill. I didn't want to tell John before he left that I wanted to brake [sic] up with him because I was afraid of what he might do. I felt bad when I saw him leaving because I don't know what is going to become of him. I was glad Tod was with him, and I hope it isn't to [sic] late to save him. . . .

I haven't told John I didn't whant [sic] him to come back to me. Do you think I should tell him now?

I want to thank all of you for being so nice to us.

Yes, I wrote her back, I thought she should tell him herself.

On Tuesday, April 11, 1972, twenty-two days after Flight 803 had arrived at Kennedy Airport with John Herndon on board, Mike Uhl arrived at the Safe Return office and called the answering service for messages. Among the handful that the operator gave him perfunctorily was the following: "Call John Herndon in Baltimore." In Baltimore! John Herndon was free!

In a frantic series of calls that followed, the facts emerged. The Pentagon had chosen to avoid a court-martial, thus avoiding a direct test on desertion in the face of war crimes; they had instead chosen to cashier John Herndon out of the service administratively, using Article 72 of the Uniform Code of Military Justice entitled "Vacation of suspension" —that is to say, General Almquist's disapproval of the bad conduct discharge was countermanded. By freeing John on a bad conduct discharge in this way, the Army ignored desertion and two-and-a-half years in exile! The Army's explanation of the matter was simply that it had taken the "appropriate" action, but our analysis was harsher: the Pentagon had buckled in the Herndon case.

When Mike conveyed the news to me, I was quickly on the phone to the Pentagon, setting up interviews for Friday, April 14. I wanted a more elaborate explanation. I would continue on up to New York Friday night for a victory celebration and buy John that pizza in Brooklyn which I had promised him in Paris as a victory present. The plan was to pick John up on the Metroliner in Baltimore. On Saturday, we would give a press conference.

At the Pentagon on Friday an Army information officer offered this explanation of their action on Herndon's case: It had been a clear, *prima facie* case of desertion, and the

Judge Advocate General, Major General George S. Prugh, had been anxious to prosecute. The JAG Corps was not intimidated, the spokesman said, by the "Nurembergy kinds of things" that the defense might offer. I was handed two memorandums from Major General Prugh, to the U.S. Army Chief of Staff, General William C. Westmoreland, one dated March 22, detailing the steps of the court actions since John's arrival on March 20; the other, cataloging previous judicial actions against John. In both memorandums the subject was: "Test Case on Amnesty for Returning Anti-War Expatriates (U.S. ex rel. John David Herndon v. Laird, Froehlke, Key)." This was one more indication that the highest levels of the Pentagon were keeping abreast of the case.

If the Judge Advocate General was enthusiastic to prosecute Herndon and felt he had a clear case of desertion, I asked who was *not* enthusiastic about prosecuting him? I never got an answer to that question.

"The purpose of military justice is to serve the military," the spokesman began (which seemed to me to be an illuminating explanation of the conduct of military justice in the Green Beret and My Lai cases). "There are only two kinds of prisoners whom it is in the interest of the military to confine: those who are a clear danger to the military community like murderers or rapists, and those who can be retrained and rehabilitated into good soldiers. Herndon did not fit either category. Therefore, it would have served no interest of the military to put Herndon in jail. Given the expense of a long trial and the expense of confinement, the Army found it inconvenient to prosecute him."

I was astounded! Would the military find it inconvenient to prosecute others like Herndon who came back in this way? I asked. The answer was, "In my opinion, yes."

After a number of other interviews on the Defense Department policy, I boarded the train and met John in Baltimore. His hair was a bit shorter, and he wore a different set of clothes for once: peach-colored pants and a gray pullover. On the way to New York, drinking a beer which he called "atrocious," and saying he couldn't wait to get to New York to buy a pack of Gauloises Filtres, he told me of his release.

"On Sunday," he said, "a guard came around and said, 'Hey Herndon, when you gettin' outta here?' and I said, 'Gettin' out pretty soon.' Then on Monday at about 2:30, a guy comes in and says, "Pack your stuff, Herndon, you're out-processin'.' I said, 'Oh, that's nice.' Figured I'd have to go to a different jail or something. Two E-7s met me and took me to an administrative building. I got a physical. The sergeants didn't say much during it. Just 'How was Paris?' and stuff like that. But after the physical one of 'em said, 'Well, I tell you what we got to do. We got to get you discharged. General Cooksey, who runs this post, said he wants you off this post today.' "

Major General Howard H. Cooksey, who had been the responsible authority in John's discharge, had indeed wanted to be rid of John fast. In adjoining Wrightstown, N.J., Terry Klug and Andy Stapp, now associated with the American Servicemen's Union and fellow graduates with John of Max's Paris School for political war resisters, were leafleting on John's case. The sergeants took John to a PX and bought him a set of civilian clothes. (Usually soldiers are given the use of a uniform for ten days after their discharge.) And they took him to Wrightstown. The buses were on strike, so John, characteristically, went to a bar. There he met two GIs, told them he had just been discharged, and offered them ten dollars to take him home.

"Before we took off, I called Mom up on the phone 'n' said, 'Hey, Mom, I'm out. I'm comin' home. Have dinner ready.' She couldn't talk. All I heard on the other end was a little racket. So I just hung up. When we came around the curve in the road near my house, Pop was standing out in the driveway."

The press conference the following morning was to be the first time that John was made available to the press since his release, but it appeared that we had overestimated the excitement about this event. Only a few reporters attended, and little appeared in print. A reporter there said we should not be disappointed at the poor attendence. It was Saturday, and the first Mets game of the season was being played at Shea Stadium. Nonetheless, it was my first opportunity to speculate on the significance of the Herndon case. That analysis has broadened and tempered since that victorious day in April 1972.

The success in John's case was a combination of six factors. First and foremost, John Herndon was the right person for the all-important case; his significance as a person goes beyond the issue of amnesty. He is a symbol of exile and what it can do to a person, but he is also a physical and psychological casualty of the war which produced the phenomenon of exile, and is representative of the kind of person that America has forced to fight its front line battle. Thus, in a fundamental sense, John Herndon is the Vietnam era incarnate. Second, the timing of the return was perfect, and completely a matter of luck. Earlier, with substantial numbers of combat troops still in Vietnam, the Army would not have been so sensitive about the issue; later, after the North Vietnamese offensive began, and the revengeful mining of Haiphong harbor by the Cyclops had taken place, and Operation Linebacker, Nixon's bombing campaign of the North was on, the peace forces were again preoccupied with resistance against the old military victory psychology. In fact, the amnesty project of the American Civil Liberties Union postponed a national conference on amnesty scheduled for May, feeling that a conference at that time would appear ridiculous to the American people. Third, Safe Return's preparedness to wage a Nuremberg defense would have made a trial long, expensive, and most of all, embarrassing for the military. Fourth, the open, publicized reentry which made no compromises with the United States military or the U.S. government put the authorities on the defensive from the beginning. Fifth, the support of anti-war senators and representatives prevented the military from burying the case in its legal machinery. And last, the availability of sign carriers and leafleteers to stage demonstrations like the one at Fort Dix in John's behalf made the case an irritant and gave it an urgency.

A new technique had been developed for a period of transition to a time when the war was truly over, and the American government recognized its postwar responsibilities. The possibility that the Herndon case opened up is *Amnesty by Default*. The Congress and the Judiciary and the military courts have defaulted throughout the Vietnam era from a consideration of the war crimes issue. For once this abrogation of responsibility could be put to use *for* the cause of the peace advocates rather than against them. The inability of American institutions to face the issue of what the United States has done in Vietnam—and, further, what it has done to its own younger generation—has been a major theme of the entire Vietnam era. If prosecuting war resisters who return openly would mean that military and civilian judicial authorities would have to confront the war crimes issue squarely, I believe they would rather evade the issue, and opt for no prosecution as the "appropriate" action.

I favor, therefore, a coalition of political and legal groups for this interim period to provide the service of prepared reentry to the refugees in exile and underground. It can only be a service, however, available to the refugee once he has already made the decision to return home. The service must in no way influence that decision. For the Herndon case sets a precedent in a political sense, not in a legal one. The Army does not have to act as it did with John Herndon, and it could turn around at any moment and decide to make a punitive example of a deserter. If, however, it tried such a vindictive act, it could only happen in the secretive recesses of the military justice system. A broad, well-organized coalition of experts could make an open prosecution very inconvenient, not ony in military court, but in civilian court as well, where the draft resisters would have to be tried.

One thing, therefore, is clear beyond doubt from the Herndon case: that it is not in the interest of any war resister in exile, regardless of how desperate his circumstances abroad have become, to return quietly on the government's terms. For until the Justice Department announces a policy on the prosecution of draft resisters, or the Congress or the President directs the Pentagon to a specific course of action on deserters *consistent* with Vietnamization, any exile will be handled by the bureaucratic dictates of the Selective Service laws or the Uniform Code of Military Justice. Amnesty is a political issue, not a legal one. Thus, until responsibilities are faced, reentry, with the goal of amnesty by default, must be politically charged.

The Herndon case proves both the possibility and the limitation of the case-by-case approach, however. It took four months of planning to bring John Herndon back and get him released. By such a standard it would take a long time to reclaim the 100,000 or so men who are thought to be in exile. Thus, there is no substitute for the over-all political solution to the amnesty question. But the surfacing of the resisters underground and the reentry of exiles which has accelerated since April 1972 will speed that broad political solution.

The over-all solution is likely to start with a suggestion of a case-by-case analysis of deserters. Such a suggestion, however, is only appropriate if there is a simultaneous case-by-case analysis of American war atrocities. Since the latter is not likely to be sponsored by this government, then the former must be fought by peace groups as completely inappropriate by any moral standard. A case-by-case approach to amnesty or to war crimes will insure a postwar period of recrimination which could last years and thus postpone a reconciliation of the country. Only with a universal amnesty can this dilatory stage be avoided. Only with universal amnesty can a meaningful reconcilation begin, a reconciliation beyond the appeasement of dissident voices, that commits the country to a substantial reordering of priorities.

Who in this country is qualified to judge John Herndon? Where would any U.S. government–sponsored agency derive its moral right to sit in judgment on whether or not his decision to desert was conscientious? What would it have meant to have forced John Herndon into three years of alternative service in a VA Hospital or to put him to work in Vista? The suggestion of such punishment is absurd. The idea of alternative service springs from the unrepentant guilty conscience of America. "Forced exile is a high enough price to pay for what I believe," John had said.

But it appears that, short of proclamation by a President

who understands that universal amnesty is the only apt action after an immoral war of this magnitude, the proposals for general amnesty will have to be taken on one by one. Even the most liberal proposal now before Congress, Bella Abzug's "War Resisters Exoneration Act of 1972," announced in a press conference to which she brought Josephine Herndon (John was still in jail), contains the unacceptable provision for an amnesty commission. The commission would have five members, paid $42,500 a year of the taxpayers' money, not to mention the further cost of office space and staff. What would be its purpose? It would be this: To afford the chance of petitioning for amnesty to any who had violated *any other law besides the Selective Service law or the Uniform Code of Military Justice* and to grant them amnesty if their law-breaking was "in substantial part" motivated by protest against the war and if the individual was "not personally responsible for any significant property damage or substantial personal injury." Who are these people that justify this magnitude of government expense? Not the bombers of the University of Wisconsin Army Laboratory, for they would have been involved in substantial property damage and substantial personal injury.

Abzug's proposal creates a phantom body of exiles who do not exist. And even if there were a body of petty thieves or small-time bombers or minor assaulters to be dealt with, to let them prevent the declaration of true universal amnesty is a case of wildly distorted emphasis. The *phenomenon* of exile is a product of the Vietnam War and the result of government policy. Any attempt by that government to ferret out the handful of true criminals among the tens of thousands of refugees is impracticable, too expensive, too time-consuming, and inappropriate morally.

Although Abzug likes to call her bill a universal amnesty proposal, it is, in effect, with the commission proviso, only a proposal for general amnesty. What is needed, as I have said before, is simply a one-sentence Universal Amnesty Declaration patterned on Andrew Johnson's Proclamation of Christmas Eve, 1868.

I, Andrew Johnson, President of the United States, by virtue of the power and authority in me vested by the Constitution, and in the name of the sovereign people of the United States, do hereby proclaim and declare unconditionally, and without reservation, to all and to every person who directly or indirectly participated in the late insurrection or rebellion, a full pardon and amnesty for the offense of treason against the United States, or of adhering to their enemies during the late civil war, with restoration of all rights, privileges and immunities under the Constitution and the laws which have been made in pursuance thereof.

But I should not be attacking the friends of amnesty. Abzug's bill is the closest thing we have to an appropriate response, and so far her bill has been ignored by press and Congress or interpreted as a competitive move against her fellow Manhattan Congressman Edward Koch, the author of the punitive proposal for two years' alternative service as the price of repatriation.

The far larger problem is to educate the American people on amnesty, and persuade them that any form of amnesty is the proper step now, let alone universal amnesty. The continued banishment of thousands of refugees abroad will prevent the American people from expunging Vietnam from its mind as quickly as it would like to do in a postwar period. It will be impossible to ignore these young men and return to business as usual. A general amnesty will not remove the exile as a prod to the American conscience, because few will come back when the price of return is the punishment of alternative service. Humanitarian alternative service is no substitute for the acceptance of a humanitarian spirit by the country itself. The country will have to prove now that *it* is worthy of respect, that it is a "great society," that it can withdraw from Vietnam with "dignity and honor" by domestic as well as foreign actions. That stance is possible only with a comprehensive policy of reconciliation which attends to *all* war victims—in South and North Vietnam, in all of North America, and in Europe.

Still, five arguments against amnesty are persistently argued:

1. *Timing.* Melvin Laird said about amnesty on February 3, 1972, "the [amnesty] question should not be considered until every young American has been returned from the prisoner-of-war camps or we have a complete accounting for every man missing in action in accordance with the Geneva Conventions, and even the enemy has signed those Conventions, and refuses to abide by them. While there's a single American involved in combat operations and being drafted into our service and going to serve his country in accordance with the laws of this nation, this is not the time for us to consider that question."

Nonsense. We are led to believe that American troops will soon be out of Indochina, and a rethinking of military aid around the world is underway. Thus, we elected, in effect, a postwar President in November 1972, whose chief task in the next four years should be the reconciliation and reconstruction of America. Thus, discussion of this issue has been appropriate for months.

2. *The viability of the military.* It is said that the draft will be untenable if its evaders and deserters are allowed to return with impunity. But in 1971, for every four young Americans who enlisted in the armed forces, one deserted. Thus, the concept of patriotic sacrifice is already thoroughly shattered by American policies, and amnesty would not affect it whatever. The real question concerning the draft in the postwar period is: Draft for what? If young men are to be drafted for further adventures like Vietnam, then such a draft should be untenable. The younger generation of Americans should reinstitute the organization of the late thirties called "Veterans of Future Wars."

3. *Waving the bloody shirt.* In the waning years of Reconstruction in the South of the early 1870s, Republican politicians found it necessary to engage in a practice known as "waving the bloody shirt," alluding to the 300,000 Union dead in the Civil War. The practice, used then to engender support for bankrupt policies by stirring up old Civil War passions, has arisen again a century later. The argument that granting amnesty would dishonor those who fought and died in Vietnam is directed against the wrong party. It is the

government who must explain to those young men who fought in Vietnam what the value of the fight was. Furthermore, to assume that those who fought will be against those who refused to fight is simply not borne out by the facts. For example, the most vital anti-war element on the campuses today is the veterans against the war. With the subsiding threat of the draft, the young college students have turned to other concerns or non-concerns. On December 24, 1971, the 103rd Anniversary of Andrew Johnson's Universal Amnesty Proclamation, veterans' groups from Pennsylvania, New York, and North Carolina presented 35,000 names on amnesty petitions to the White House. The special bitterness of the anti-war veteran today is lodged in his realization that he was sent off by his country to risk his life in an illegitimate cause. He was, in short, conned into fighting.

The more brutal and presumptuous side of this argument is the use of the 55,000 dead as a block to amnesty. Dalton Trumbo in *Johnny Got His Gun* spoke most pointedly to this argument.

> You can always hear the people who are willing to sacrifice somebody else's life. They're plenty loud and they talk all the time. You can find them in churches and schools and newspapers and legislatures and congress. That's their business. They sound wonderful. Death before dishonor. This ground sanctified by blood. These men who died so gloriously They shall not have died in vain. Our noble dead.
> Hmmmm.
> But what do the dead say?
> Did anybody ever come back from the dead, any single one of the millions who got killed, did any one of them ever come back and say, by god I'm glad I'm dead because death is always better than dishonor? Did they say I'm glad I died to make the world safe for democracy? Did they say I like death better than losing liberty? Did any of them ever say it's good to think I got my guts blown out for the honor of my country? Did any of them ever say, look at me, I'm dead but I died for decency and that's better than being alive? Did any of them ever say, here I am I've been rotting for two years in a foreign grave

but it's wonderful to die for your native land? Did any of them say, Hurray I died for womanhood and I'm happy see how I sing even though my mouth is choked with worms.

Nobody but the dead know whether all these things people talk about are worth dying for or not. And the dead can't talk....

4. *What do you say to the families of the dead, wounded, or captured?* On the December 12, 1971, "Sixty Minutes" show on CBS, Mike Wallace (who often evinces insensitivity for human feelings) said to the mother of an exile, "And to the mothers and fathers of the kids who fought and some of them were wounded and some of them died, what do you say to them?" The lady attempted to answer and then broke down in sobs.

Since when is it the responsibility of the exile or his family to offer any explanation to the wounded or the families of these other victims? It is the government's job to do that. To deny amnesty will not confer any more meaning on the deaths of the 55,000 or on the plight of the wounded or captured, nor should it console their families any more.

Underlying this argument by the adversaries of amnesty is the misconception that the families of the dead, wounded, or captured will be opposed to amnesty. This is doubtful. No one knows. They have not been polled. But at the Kennedy amnesty hearings February 28, 1972, two dramatic testimonies indicated a mixed reaction.

Mrs. Valerie Kushner, the wife of a prisoner held in captivity for over four years, pointed out that POWs and war resisters were both unwilling exiles:

"I would ask you to open your hearts to the words of Ecclesiastes," she said. " 'To everything there is a season, and a time to every purpose under the heaven ... a time to kill, and a time to heal; a time to break down, and a time to build up.' We have had our time of killing and now we must prepare ourselves for the time of healing. We cannot expect to make whole the body America if we amputate from her flesh so many of her sons."

And Robert Ransom, whose son, Mike, was killed in Vietnam in 1968, testified: "... the untenable position into which we forced these young men is responsible for their predicament today. These are our sons, and we need them back. They did not deserve what we have done to them. It would be most gratifying to me if I felt that I could have contributed in any small measure toward the granting of the broadest kind of amnesty—one without penalties and conditions. I would consider it to be my personal Mike Ransom Memorial General Amnesty Bill. That would have pleased him."

5. *Why scot-free?* The final retreat of those who desire to avoid the true issue of amnesty is the argument that the exiles have violated the law, and they must pay for it. Scotfree would be scoff-law. This has given the impetus to the sentiment for conditional amnesty with its punitive proposals of alternative service.

But who has been the supreme lawbreaker in this era? How many Americans shudder when they hear their own President speak of "the international outlaws in Hanoi?" America did not declare war in Vietnam, but it was responsible for the Nuremberg tribunal, at which it ratified a whole category of crime entitled Crimes against Humanity—extermination, enslavement, deportation, and other inhumane acts committed against a civilian population. After eight years of American involvement, there are one million civilian casualties and six million refugees in South Vietnam, and one-fourth of the Cambodian population was made refugees after three months of our invasion there, which the Administration called a success. And Laos is the most heavily bombed country in the history of land warfare. Robert Jackson, the chief prosecutor of the Nuremberg trials said: "If certain acts in violation of treaties are crimes, they are crimes whether the United States does them or whether Germany does them, and we are not prepared to lay down a rule of criminal conduct against others which we would be unwilling to invoke against ourselves." So let us not hear any longer this selective application of the "respect for the law" argument invoked for the exile, but not for the government of the United States.

Universal amnesty subsumes repatriation with the acceptance of responsibility for the war. It would be an act of the soul and of the spirit. It would show a moral strength in our country. It offers a new start; it commits the country to define the lessons of the war, and to act upon those lessons, so that this will never happen again. Conditional amnesty offers repatriation without the guilt; a return to acceptance of business as usual. It evinces no largeness of spirit, bears not at all on the quality of moral strength, and has no reference to the substantive changes that are required in American foreign policy.

Exile is penalty enough. It is a self-imposed alternative service. For this government to add an additional penalty would be a cowardly act, contemptuous of the past, unrelated to a new beginning, and one that the exiles have made very clear that they will not accept.

In early June, two months after his release from the Fort Dix stockade, John Herndon stayed with me for three days in North Carolina. His mother had said several weeks before that when she first saw her son at Kennedy Airport, he "looked so thin, like he'd been strung all the way from Paris to New York." Mrs. Herndon had set to work on the problem since John had been home. He had gained fifteen pounds, and his waistline was 32 instead of 30, and "still expanding." (In October of 1972 he weighed 178 pounds, 36 pounds heavier than his Paris weight.) If John refused food around home, his mother would say, "Your protestin' don't mean nothin' around here." Health was a good place to start in reclaiming John.

He had had a hectic two months in the public eye. He'd traveled to Boston and Philadelphia; he'd testified before a Congressional committee on "Racism in the Uniform Code of Military Justice"; he'd been the star of a fund-raising party for Safe Return and had been on television in Baltimore and New York. Now he was coming South where his sympathizers were fewer, traveling on a grant from the organization "Resist" to the anti-war bookshop at Camp Lejeune and the Quaker House near Fort Bragg. In Chapel Hill, the North Carolina Veterans for Peace, who had sponsored a universal amnesty petition in the fall, were giving a party for him.

John was brimming with ideas for political events that might dramatize the plight of the exile. His own plight was shared by 101,399 other servicemen who since 1966 had been discharged from military service with undesirable, bad conduct, or dishonorable discharges. With his bad conduct discharge he would have trouble getting a job, and he was denied all veterans' benefits. He was not entitled to unemployment compensation, reemployment rights, or civil service preference under the Department of Labor's program for veterans, nor to vocational rehabilitation or educational assistance under the Veterans Administration. Nor was he eligible to have his discharge reviewed by the Army Discharge Review Board. He had been in touch with Bella Abzug's office on this denial of rights.

John's visit to Fort Bragg had followed that of Staff Sergeant George Smith, who had spent two years in captivity with the NLF and who had been released by them as a gesture of respect to Norman Morrison, a Quaker who burned himself to death at the Pentagon in 1965 in protest against the war. Smith had said at Fort Bragg, "... the longer the war continues, the more the POWs will suffer, as Vietnamese continue to suffer and die from American bombs and electronic battlefields." John wanted to get in touch with Smith, who is now a rural mail carrier in West Virginia, and propose that they give a joint press conference to show "solidarity" between the two groups of exiles. He had also been in touch with a liberal judge in Baltimore about declaring an amnesty for war resisters within the city limits of Baltimore as Berkeley had done, and was also considering joining the V.F.W. to confront it on amnesty.

While I was interested in these political actions and approved of them all as useful and creative, I was more interested in John's future as a person. He was my friend now, and I felt a certain fraternal responsibility for him in freedom. The identity of a deserter is no identity on which to base one's sense of personal worth in America. It is not the sort of posture upon which maturity can develop healthily. John had left his country when he was an adolescent, testing his virility, and had been in extraordinary circumstances ever since. He had seldom had to take responsibility for his actions. His circumstances had dictated them. He was essentially still that adolescent who had left, with his hip talk and his bar-room braggadocio. John needed to establish a more normal coexistence with the world, with a job and a steady income and a place to live; to relate to people without reference to desertion or resistance. I wanted to see him lose the cunning of the survivor that was still evident in his face and in his cautious approach to people. He talked endlessly about Vietnam and Paris and Annette. He complained that he could not communicate with people in this country. They could not understand what he had been through or they seemed embarrassed to hear about it. Only the people in "the movement" were interested.

He was an important figure to the amnesty movement now, but what would happen to him later, when amnesty was not on people's minds any longer? He would be in great demand in the coming months, but without a job and without going back to school for his General Equivalence Degree, he was as much in danger of being used in freedom as he was in exile or in the Army. So we talked about a job and an education. He was interested, saying he intended to do both "when things slow down a little," and he seemed flattered that I would be so concerned.

He wanted me know that his adjustment was already beginning. "I can already tell the difference," he said, "I'm much more relaxed. When I'm with women, I'm much gentler, and when I'm drinkin', I don't get hostile like I used to."

Annette had finally written him. They were parting as friends. She had written that she would like to meet him again someday under normal circumstances. She had asked John to go to Philadelphia for her and get depositions from her family for the custody case. John would go later.

"Of course, I'll remember her for the rest of my life," he said, "and her, me, I'm pretty sure. Once she gets custody of the kid, I'm sure she'll write me a letter, regardless if she's living with somebody else or married or by herself. If she ever wants money to come back to the United States, I'll send it to her regardless of whether I'm married and have kids or not. I'll always feel I owe her that. She did so much for me when I was over there. I would never deny her the right to come back. If she wants to come back and can't afford it, I'll make it possible for her."

John went off to bed that night with a bottle of scotch, mixing with iced tea, the only mixer in our icebox, and made some notes on his stay in the South. The following day he repaired the radio in my battered Volkswagen and explored Cane Creek nearby for good fishing spots. He seemed perfectly happy to putter around the place—agreeable to nearly any suggestion I made, unhurried and relaxed, his fuller face having lost some of its Paris tension. In the early evening he packed his small blue suitcase, and we went to Raleigh, where he was to appear on a statewide call-in show. I expected that the show would be pretty rough, and it was.

The program began with John giving a short synopsis of his travels, and it was settled that he had no qualms about being called a deserter. Then the moderator set the tone of the rest of the program.

"Did you have a relative in World War II?"

"Yes, my father."

"Did it ever occur to you that if he had deserted, we'd all be speaking Japanese or German today?"

And shortly later, the moderator asked, "Why did you come back?"

"France is not my country," John began, "America is my country. . . ."

"That's questionable," his host broke in.

The onslaught of calls began timidly with a woman.

"I don't think this fellow should be so proud of his desertion. I think he should be proud to be in the United States and be willing to serve in armed services. I'm not proud of him at all. It's better that he is out, because I don't want him over there supporting me with the attitude he has. . . ."

And then the calls began to take more of a bite.

Husky male voice: "I wonder if I could ask this traitor two questions: Why did he reenlist, and, as a war criminal and a traitor, what's he doing for a livelihood now?"

Middle-aged male: "I'm surprised that WPTF would have somebody like this character on the air."

"Well, sir, we thought it might be enlightening ... as an educational experience," the moderator replied.

"It's enlightening, but it's not very educational."

"It might be educational in a different way from what you're thinking about," the moderator said airily.

World War II veteran: "I was in World War II and I didn't have a chance to run and hide somewhere."

"Neither did my father," John said, "but he backed me 100 percent."

"I think anyone who's chicken enough to run out, whatever the country wanted to do with them, declared war or not ... I think he should go to bat for em. That's my opinion. I don't want to talk to him."

Young woman: "If they're going to desert their country, how can we trust 'em to be over here?"

Older woman: "Well, you know what my theory is. If they don't like their country, leave it. He has a right to his opinion too. But don't come back and enjoy the comforts of our country, and condemn our government. As bad as it may be, they say it's the best one in the world. When they do things like this, they play into the hands of the Communists."

"I agree with that," the moderator said.

Middle-aged woman: "You say you're working for an organization. May I ask who's putting up the money for this organization, and I don't want you to tell me just plain ordinary citizens?"

Middle-aged woman: "I would have to call him a traitor also. I would like to know what he hopes to accomplish by doing this. If he were in Red China and had the views he has, he would have already been put before a firing squad and filled with bullets."

But John was enjoying himself. How different this was from the New York-Boston-Baltimore shows that he had been on! Was it more reflective of how the country as a whole feels about amnesty for deserters? John had never been asked before if he approved of prayers in school or saluting the flag in school, or of the Communists' method of operation. The sympathetic discussions were getting to be a bore, but this was fun!

Masculine voice: "Do you advocate the overthrow of this great country?"

John: "We're not trying to overthrow the country. We're just trying to straighten it out."

"Well, I don't think you're straightening it out with the attitude that. . ."

John: "Well, apparently, we're doin' some good, 'cause we're getting a lot of telephone calls here tonight, and a lot of people are going to take a different attitude than the ones who called in."

College student: "Are you an isolationist?"

John: "Who's isolated?"

He was becoming a master at putting the questioner on the defensive. A man was talking about the devastation he had seen in Europe after the Second World War as a member of the merchant marine, saying he would die before his children had to experience that kind of poverty.

"Have you ever been in exile, sir?" John asked.

"No."

"Then you really don't know what it's all about, do you?"

"I think I do."

"Thinking and knowing is two different things. I spent fifteen months in Vietnam so I know what Vietnam is like. I know what Paris is like. And I know what the United States is like because I was born here."

"Well, Nixon is doin' his dead-level best to get us out of Vietnam, and I challenge anyone to prove me wrong."

"If you were in Red China or Russia or North Vietnam, you wouldn't be able to talk like this over the radio."

John: "I'd sure try, ma'am. I'd sure try."

Tremulous teenage male: "Would you ask your guest if he thinks he's settin a good example for the American people by doing what he's doing."

John: "I'm giving the American people something to look at from my side of the story, from a guy that's been there, and a guy that's left, and a guy that's come back, 'cause he wants to get some things straightened out with the government."

"Do you think of yourself as a patriotic citizen?"

John: "Yes, I am patriotic. If something happened within the United States, I'd be more than happy to go back into the service."

"But every war we've fought has been a war that nobody likes. There have been the conscientious objectors, even men who bore arms, and fought and died in battle. To me a person who will not bear arms against an enemy of his country has relinquished his right to be an American citizen."

John: "The Vietnamese people are not fighting here. They are fighting over there."

"Every traitor has been coldly received in any country he's gone to..."

John: "Not in Sweden, France, Canada, Holland..."

"But look at England..."

John: "There's American deserters in England and Ireland, and Spain, and Italy; in fact, in every country in Europe. And they're doing O.K. They're surviving."

"They're surviving, but are they living well?"

John: "You're surviving, aren't you? Have you ever been in Vietnam?"

"No."

"Then you really don't know what goes on in a war, do you?"

"No, but..."

"Well, I've been wounded three times over there. And I've seen guys laying there beside me who've had their legs blown off and their arms blown off, and they were laying there protestin' the war, because they didn't know what the hell they were over there fightin' for."

In the hour of relentless assault on John, only one caller came to his defense. The male voice sounded young and there was a foreign lilt to it.

"People have suggested that Mr. Herndon has been acting cowardly. I don't think I would be brave enough to go through what he's gone through. It's more of the coward's position to stay in the war if you're against it."

Moderator: "It depends whether you'd rather be taunted on the street or shot at."

"A lot of people are fighting over there because they're

afraid to face the consequences of doing what is right. And Mr. Herndon is a brave individual, and a very free individual, free in his own soul, At least that's the way he sounds."

I felt as if I had to console John after it was over. I had never met anyone who would not have been completely worn out and despairing after such an ordeal, and John, I thought, would need his confidence bolstered. But when I got to him he was absolutely exhilarated—and why not? He knew he was right. He chuckled at the memory of it, and talked about his technique of throwing questions back at them. It was if he had discovered a new country and conquered it.

We hustled out of the station. Across the street in a parking lot, a large man glowered at us intently, holding a stick in his hand. But he made no motions toward us.

"A man could get killed in Raleigh," John chortled when we were safely away.

Who was this man, John Herndon? Where did he get the strength and the confidence to stand up against such abuse, even to take it with a sense of humor? I was full of admiration for him. I had been inclined from the beginning to think of him as a dispossessed person whose country had piled unmanageable woes upon him, the victim of circustances that I had talked about with Mike and Tod in those early December discussions, Maria's social case. But this was a man and a symbol that the country would have to deal with now.

"We do not want to be welcomed back as moral heroes," a deserter in Canada had said a month earlier, "just as ordinary citizens." And yet who have been hereos to America in the past? Often in past wars they have been men from John's background. There have been an inordinate number of Medal of Honor winners from the Appalachian mountains (as well as an inordinate number of racing car drivers), and John is more Appalachian than Baltimorian. The mountains breed many courageous people, though some call them reckless. John's performance that night and many nights to come was courageous, but was it reckless as well? It was a question for me, not John, for he had his mission now. He met Thomas Carlyle's first test of a hero: sincerity.

The country's view of a hero has changed in the Vietnam

era. When in May of 1972 the Navy acquired its first aces of the war, two pilots who had shot down five MIGs over North Vietnam, the celebrations were curiously flat. It was as if the country recognized, at least tacitly, that the real war heroes were on the ground, and not Caucasian. We would probably never know the tales of superhuman effort in the face of American laser beams and saturation strikes, or if we did, we would surely call them propaganda.

Would John's case be recognized as a triumph of the spirit, or would he be "taunted on the street?" The Raleigh program was one indication. Anyway, it did not matter to John. He would "do his thing" cheerfully.

I put him on a bus in Raleigh. It was an overnight trip to Augusta, Georgia, near Fort Gordon, where Lewis Plyler was about to be tried for desertion. He was the deserter who had lived with John and Annette in Paris for a month, who had left a bill at the local café and told the owner that John would pay it, whose action had almost eventuated in John's suicide. John was going down to investigate the case for Safe Return, to find out about what legal help Lewis had, and what strategy his defense would follow.

It was his generosity, his hard-won generosity that was coming to the surface once again. But would this quality last forever in his new circumstance at home? Would the American people make a place for the war resisters in the postwar period? Or would they maintain a hostile hypocrisy toward them? Would war resistance in the seventies become a badge of honor in time, akin to civil rights resistance in the sixties, respected by the public as a difficult and courageous lot? Would the American people ever recognize the moral debt they owe to the resisters?

"He's in trouble now," John said of Plyler. "I know if I was in trouble, and he was in a position to help, he'd do it. That was a different circumstance in Paris. You did what you had to in order to survive. What he did over there is not important now."

No, the important thing was what would happen at home.

ALVERNO COLLEGE LIBRARY
The amnesty of John David Herndon
959.704R436

2 5050 00260832 7

99807

REMOVED FROM THE
ALVERNO COLLEGE LIBRARY

959.704
R 436

Alverno College Library
Milwaukee, Wisconsin